Beginners' Russian

Rachel Farmer

Revised by Tanya Linaker

First published in Great Britain in 1996 as *Teach Yourself Beginners' Russian* by Hodder Education. An Hachette UK company.

This edition published by Teach Yourself in 2025.
An imprint of John Murray Press.

1

Editorial support from Haremi Ltd.

A CIP catalogue record for this title is available from the British Library.

Paperback ISBN 978 1 399 81825 4
ebook ISBN 978 1 399 81928 2

Typeset by Integra Software Services Pvt. Ltd., Pondicherry, India.

Printed and bound in Great Britain by Clays Ltd, Elcograf S.p.A.

John Murray Press policy is to use papers that are natural, renewable and recyclable products and made from wood grown in sustainable forests. The logging and manufacturing processes are expected to conform to the environmental regulations of the country of origin.

John Murray Press
Carmelite House
50 Victoria Embankment
London EC4Y 0DZ

123 S. Broad St., Ste 2750
Philadelphia, PA 19109

www.teachyourself.com

John Murray Press, part of Hodder & Stoughton Limited.
An Hachette UK company.

The authorised representative in the EEA is Hachette Ireland,
8 Castlecourt Centre, Dublin 15, D15 XTP3, Ireland (email: info@hbgi.ie)

Contents

About the author

I graduated in Russian, French and Serbo-Croat at the University of Birmingham, and then gained a teaching qualification at the University of Nottingham.

I went on to teach languages, particularly Russian, to learners in schools, colleges, prisons: anywhere I could inspire and cultivate an interest in the Russian language and culture. For ten years I taught Russian at the University of Nottingham, during which time I wrote my PhD thesis on the Russian writer Voinovich, who became a lifelong friend.

Over the years I have visited and worked in Russia at every opportunity and now deliver training and coaching in cross-cultural issues, and leadership and management to national and international managers in Russian-speaking countries. I also train, coach and carry out research for European businesses which have links with Russia.

Russia has exerted a strong influence on my life ever since I first studied the language at school, and it colors many of my interests. I have always loved reading, especially Russian fiction, and I enjoy writing fiction myself, with a Russian flavor of course. My other interests include travel, walking, cinema, family and friends. I am based in Nottingham.

How to use this book

This book consists of an introductory **Pronunciation guide** to familiarize you with the basic sounds of Russian and an **Introduction to Russian**, which introduces the alphabet and teaches the fundamentals of reading and writing Russian. The core of the book is 10 units which will help you learn basic language function and introduce key topics for everyday communication.

A little goes a long way!

Try to use the book little and often, rather than for long stretches at a time. This will help you to create a study habit, much in the same way you would a sport or music. Leave the book somewhere handy so that you can pick it up for just a few minutes.

Before you start, make a plan!

Setting goals affects the programming of your brain, strengthening neural pathways and ultimately making it more likely that you will achieve those goals. Before you begin, think about how much time you want to devote to learning, which skills or areas you want to focus on, and identify specific ideas you want to be able to communicate or activities you want to engage in.

Track your progress!

Start a notebook to use for study, where you can create vocabulary lists, a grammar summary, questions you'd like answered, etc. Keep track of your resources—films, podcasts, songs or blogs you like, and jot down a few words or expressions you may have recognized or learned. The more you can reflect on your learning process, the deeper your connection with the language will be. For guidance in this process, we recommend Teach Yourself's *Fluentish: Language Learning Planner & Journal* by Jo Franco.

Use the tools at the beginning of each unit to help you set goals, plan your time, and keep track of the work you do.

IN THIS UNIT, YOU WILL LEARN HOW TO

Each unit begins with an overview of the language you will be learning and skills you will be acquiring.

MY PROGRESS TRACKER

Use the progress tracker to plan your study time and to keep a record of what you've accomplished. The first column tracks time, and the remaining 5 columns represent the skills you'll be working on: listening, pronunciation, reading, writing, and spoken interaction.

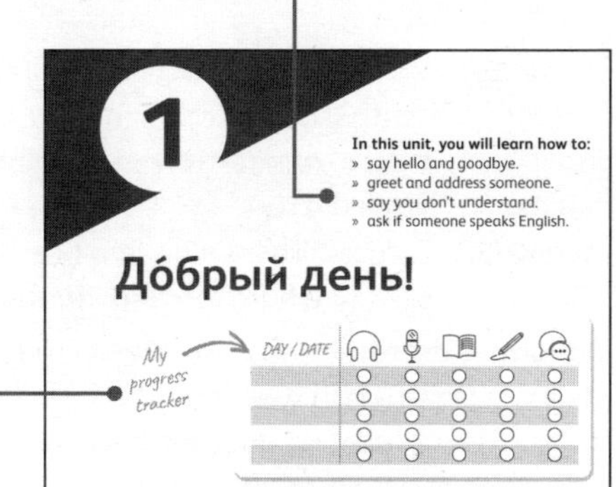

Personalize the tracker: Instead of the date or day, you can enter an increment of time. Add columns for culture, vocabulary, grammar or any other area you wish to focus on. Give yourself a star when you feel you've done particularly well. Make it your own! Review your tracker regularly and see which areas could use more practice.

Use the **Self check** at the end of each unit to evaluate your progress.

Try to practice each skill every day.

The icons in the progress tracker are used throughout the book to help you easily identify and locate the skills you want to practice:

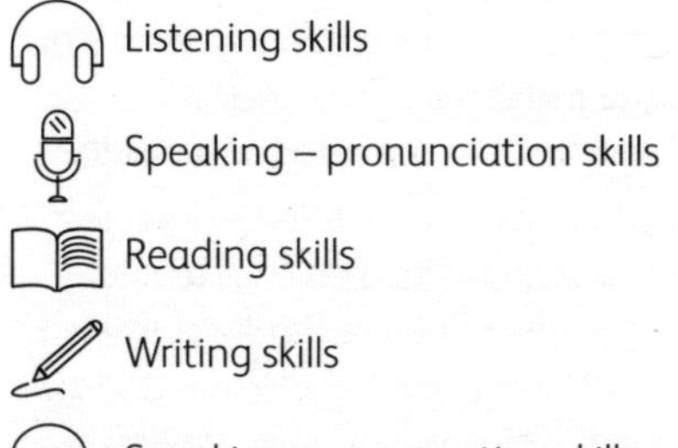

Remember: there are many ways to build your skills in addition to those provided in this book: use a language-learning app, listen to music or podcasts, watch TV shows or movies, go to a restaurant, follow social media accounts in Russian (there are wonderful teachers who post regularly), read blogs, newspapers or magazines, switch the language settings in your apps to Russian, or sign up for a language exchange or a tutor.

UNITS 1–10

The units open with a **cultural reading** in English and a **Vocabulary builder** page with thematic groupings of related words that can be studied together, as well as **new expressions** – specific words and expressions needed to understand the upcoming conversations or reading passages. You will often notice missing words in the Vocabulary builder. Look for patterns to help you complete the lists.

Dialogues are recorded conversations that you can listen to and practice, beginning with a narrative that helps you understand what you are going to hear, with a focusing question and follow-up activities. It is important to listen to or read this material at least twice; work out the meaning for yourself as far as you can, but use the lists of key words and phrases to help you. As in any conversation, listen for the meaning and don't worry about understanding each individual word. This will come with time. The **Russian–English Glossary** at the back of the book allows you to quickly access all the vocabulary that is presented in the course, and a **Transliteration appendix** presents the dialogues in the Romanized version of Cyrillic. Use it to help you as you learn the Russian writing system.

Language discovery asks you to think about one or more aspects of the language used in the dialogues. (See below for more information about the learning approach known as the Discovery method.) Key features and patterns of the language are presented throughout, accompanied by notes to guide you and draw your attention to interesting language or culture points. A **Summary of language patterns** at the back of the book shows examples of the mechanics of constructing sentences in Russian.

The **Practice** sections give you the opportunity to try out the language that has been presented in the unit; each exercise focuses on listening, reading, writing and speaking. Finally, in every unit there is a short test – **Test yourself** – which enables you to check whether you can now do some of the language tasks covered by that unit. There are also two **Reviews**, after Units 5 and 10, to help you consolidate what you've learned. You can check all your answers in the **Answer key** at the back of the book.

Revise each unit until you can do it without errors before you go on to the next unit. It is important to go back over material in areas where you are making errors, rather than carrying on regardless, which is bound to get you into trouble later.

How to be a successful language learner

The Discovery method

There are lots of philosophies and approaches to language learning, some practical, some quite unconventional, and far too many to list here. Perhaps you know of a few, or even have some techniques of your own. In this book we have incorporated the Discovery method of learning, a sort of DIY approach to language learning. What this means is that you will be encouraged throughout the course to engage your mind and figure out the language for yourself, through identifying patterns, understanding grammar concepts, noticing words that are similar to English, and more.

Simply put, if you figure something out for yourself, you're more likely to understand it. And when you use what you've learned, you're more likely to remember it. And because many of the essential but (let's admit it!) dull details, such as grammar rules, are introduced through the Discovery method, you'll have more fun while learning. Soon, the language will start to make sense and you'll be relying on your own intuition to construct original sentences independently, not just listening and repeating.

Everyone can succeed in learning a language – the key is to know how to learn it.

Learn to Learn

There are many strategies that can help you become a successful language learner. Different people have different learning styles and some of these approaches will be more effective for you than others. Use this list as a point of inspiration when you want to find the most effective ways to advance your skills and begin your journey to fluency.

VOCABULARY

Words are the building blocks of language. The more you use the words you're introduced to, the more quickly they'll lodge into your memory. These study tips will help you remember better:

- Say the words out loud as you read them. Listen to the audio several times.
- Write the words over and over again. Create flash cards, drawings and mind maps. It helps to group new words in categories, like food or furniture, or according to the situations in which they occur, e.g. restaurant, hotel, sight-seeing, or their functions, e.g. greetings, parting, thanks, apologizing.
- Cover up the English side of the vocabulary list and see if you remember the meaning of the word. Then cover up the Russian side, and do the same.
- Use mnemonic tricks with similar sounding words in English.
- Post sticky notes for words for objects around your house.
- Pay attention to patterns in words, e.g. if you know that the Russian word for information is информация (**informátsiya**), what do you think the Russian word for organization might be? It's организация (**organizátsiya**). Do you see a pattern? You can associate the -ация (-**átsiya**) ending in Russian with the English -tion.

GRAMMAR

Grammar gives your language structure. It allows you to experiment with the vocabulary you learn because you'll understand how it works together to create meaning. In other words, you'll begin to develop a feel for the language. Here are some tips to help you study more effectively:

- Write your own grammar glossary and add new information and examples as you go along.
- Experiment with grammar rules. Use known vocabulary to practice new grammar structures. Try to find examples of grammar in conversations or other articles.
- When you learn a new word, consider what other words you can turn it into. Could you turn a verb into a noun or an adjective into a verb if you apply what you know?
- When you learn a new verb form, review other verbs you know that follow the same pattern.
- Compare Russian structures with your own language or other languages you may already speak. Try to find out some rules on your own and be ready to spot the exceptions.

PRONUNCIATION

The best way to improve your pronunciation is simply to practice as much as possible. Study individual sounds first, then full words and sentences. Don't forget, it's not just about pronouncing letters and words correctly, but using the right intonation. So, when practicing words and sentences, mimic the rising and falling intonation of native speakers.

- Repeat all of the conversations, line by line. Listen to yourself and try to mimic what you hear.
- Record yourself and compare yourself to the recordings.
- Make a list of words that give you trouble and practice them.

LISTENING AND READING

The conversations in this book include questions to help guide you in your understanding. But you can go further by following some of these tips.

- Imagine the situation. Try to imagine where the scene is taking place and who the main characters are. Let your experience of the world help you guess the meaning of the conversation, e.g. if a conversation takes place in a café, you can predict the kind of vocabulary that will be used.
- Concentrate on the main part. When watching a film in another language you usually get the meaning of the whole story from a few individual scenes. Understanding a conversation or text in another language is similar. Concentrate on the main message and don't worry about individual words.
- Learn to cope with uncertainty—don't over-use your dictionary! You don't have to look up every word you don't know—try to deduce the meaning from context. Concentrate on trying to get the gist of the passage and underline the words you don't understand. If after the third time there are still words which prevent you from getting the general meaning of the passage, look them up in the dictionary.

WRITING

You'll be able to practice writing using this book, but take advantage of other opportunities to practice.

- Write out the answers to all Practice and Test Yourself questions.
- Create your own vocabulary lists and a grammar summary.
- Look up writing prompts for language learning or try writing a daily gratitude journal in Russian.
- Write out your To Do and shopping lists in Russian.
- Join online forums and discussion groups about or in Russian.

SPEAKING

The greatest obstacle to speaking a new language is the fear of making a mistake. Keep in mind that you make mistakes in your own language—it's simply part of the human condition. Accept it. Most errors are not serious and they will not affect the meaning. So concentrate on getting your message across and use the mistakes as learning opportunities. Here are some useful tips to help you practice speaking Russian:

- Rehearse in Russian. Hold a conversation with yourself, using the conversations of the units as models and the structures you have learnt previously.
- When you're going about your day, e.g. buying groceries, ordering food and drinks, do it with Russian in your mind! Look at objects around you and try to name them in Russian. Look at people around you and try to describe them in detail.
- Answer all of the questions in the book out loud. Say the dialogues out loud, then try to replace sentences with ones that are true for you. Try to role-play different situations in the book.
- Keep talking. The best way to improve your fluency in a language is to talk every time you have the opportunity to do so: keep the conversations flowing and don't worry about the mistakes. If you get stuck for a particular word, don't let the conversation stop; simplify what you want to say; paraphrase or replace the unknown word with one you do know.

Learning a language takes work. But the work can be a lot of fun! So, let's begin!

Давайте начнём! (***Davayte nachnyom***!)

Let's get started!

Pronunciation guide

Most English speakers can pronounce most Russian sounds without difficulty. What's more, reading Russian is often easier than reading English with its complicated spelling, e.g. *enough*, *plough*, *cough*. In Russian, what you see is more or less what you get, and if you join together the sound of the individual letters you will usually end up with the sound of the whole word. Here is a quick reference guide to help you.

CONSONANTS

Б	б	**b**	as in *bag*
В	в	**v**	as in *visitor*
Г	г	**g**	as in *good*
Д	д	**d**	as in *duck*
Ж	ж	**zh**	as in *pleasure*
З	з	**z**	as in *zoo*
К	к	**k**	as in *kiss*
Л	л	**l**	as in *lane*
М	м	**m**	as in *moon*
Н	н	**n**	as in *note*
П	п	**p**	as in *pin*
Р	р	**r**	as in *rabbit*
С	с	**s**	as in *sit*
Т	т	**t**	as in *tennis*
Ф	ф	**f**	as in *funny*
Х	х	**ch**	as in *loch*
Ц	ц	**ts**	as in *cats*
Ч	ч	**ch**	as in *chicken*
Ш	ш	**sh**	as in *ship*
Щ	щ	**sch**	as in *borsch*

When you listen to spoken Russian, you may notice that the first six consonants in the list will change their sound if they occur at the end of a word. Don't worry about this, but try to get into the habit of imitating the way that Russians speak.

Б	б	**b**	at the end of a word sounds like *p*
В	в	**v**	at the end of a word sounds like *f*
Г	г	**g**	at the end of a word sounds like *k*
Д	д	**d**	at the end of a word sounds like *t*
Ж	ж	**zh**	at the end of a word sounds like *sh*
З	з	**z**	at the end of a word sounds like *s*

VOWELS

If a word has more than one syllable there will be one vowel which is pronounced more strongly than the others. This is called a stressed vowel. When vowels are stressed they are pronounced clearly and strongly. When they are in an unstressed position they are pronounced more weakly. Listen to the recording whenever possible and notice what happens to vowels in different positions as you repeat the words.

А	а	**a**	as in *father*
Е	е	**ye**	as in *yesterday*
Ё	ё	**yo**	as in *yonder*
И	и	**ee**	as in *street*
Й	й	**y**	as in *toy*
О	о	**o**	as in *born*
У	у	**oo**	as in *boot*
	ы		sounds rather like *i* in *ill* (say it by keeping your mouth very slightly open and drawing your tongue back as far as it will go)
Э	э	**e**	as in *leg*
Ю	ю	**yoo**	as in *universe*
Я	я	**ya**	as in *yard*

THE SOFT AND HARD SIGNS

ь The soft sign has the effect of softening the preceding consonant, as if adding a soft *y* sound to it.

ъ The hard sign is rare, is not pronounced and makes a tiny pause between syllables.

Introduction to Russian

The Russian alphabet is called the Cyrillic alphabet after the monk, St Cyril, who invented it. In order to follow this course, you will need to know how to read Russian in its printed form. Part 1 of the introduction presents the alphabet, divided into four groups. Say the letters and words out loud and complete the practices for each group until you are fairly confident, then you will be ready to move on to another group of letters. Part 2 introduces the basic mechanics of the language for reading and writing.

Part 1: The Russian alphabet

The Russian alphabet has 33 letters. These can be divided into four groups.

GROUP 1: ENGLISH LOOK- AND SOUND-ALIKES

00.01 The first group consists of those which look and sound like their English counterparts. It contains five letters:

А	а	sounds like	*a*	in	*father*
Т	т	sounds like	*t*	in	*tennis*
О	о	sounds like	*o*	in	*born*
М	м	sounds like	*m*	in	*moon*
К	к	sounds like	*k*	in	*kiss*

With these letters you can already read the following Russian words:

áтом	*atom*	мáма	*mum*	кот	*cat*

You will notice that a diacritical mark has been used for the first vowel, the letter а, in áтом and мáма. This is to show you which syllable to emphasize in words of more than one syllable. Remember that every syllable has a vowel and it is the vowel sound that has the diacritical mark to show you the correct stress. In English, if we marked every stressed syllable, it would look like this: the piáno pláyer wants to recórd a récord.

When you are speaking Russian, put lots of energy into the stressed syllable and pronounce it clearly. The vowels in unstressed syllables are underplayed and do not need to be pronounced so clearly. For example, in the syllable before the stress, *o* will sound like *a* in *father*, and in any other position it will sound like *a* in *asleep*. You will soon get used to where the stress falls on words which you use often, but to help you the stress will be shown throughout the book.

GROUP 2: FALSE FRIENDS

00.02 The letters in this group look like English letters but sound different. The group contains seven letters:

С	с	sounds like	*s*	in	*sit*
Р	р	sounds like	*r*	in	*rabbit*
Е	е	sounds like	*ye*	in	*yesterday* (when unstressed, like *yi* or *i*)
В	в	sounds like	*v*	in	*visitor*
Н	н	sounds like	*n*	in	*note*
У	у	sounds like	*oo*	in	*boot*
Х	х	sounds like	*ch*	in	*loch* (Scots)

PRACTICE

00.03 **Listen to the audio first then complete the activity.**

1 Match the cities in English and Russian.

a Томск — **1** Vienna
b Торóнто — **2** Tomsk
c Вéна — **3** Murmansk
d Омск — **4** Toronto
e Мýрманск — **5** Omsk

2 **Try to match these Russian names with their English equivalents.**

a	Свéта	**1**	Anna
b	Антóн	**2**	Vyera
c	Вéра	**3**	Sveta
d	Ромáн	**4**	Anton
e	Áнна	**5**	Roman

3 **And now match these signs.**

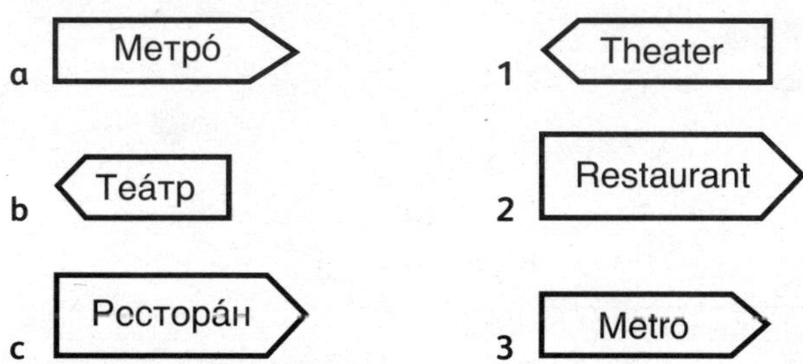

4 **Your Russian friend gives you a shopping list. Match the Russian and English translations.**

a	сóус	**1**	cocoa
b	какáо	**2**	sauce
c	сáхар	**3**	rum
d	ром	**4**	sugar

00.04 GROUP 3A: UNFAMILIAR LETTERS WITH FAMILIAR SOUNDS. PART 1.

The next group of letters contains 13 new letters and is divided here into three parts: A–C. Here are the first five:

П	п	sounds like	*p*	in	*pin*
Л	л	sounds like	*l*	in	*lane*
И	и	sounds like	*ee*	in	*street*
З	з	sounds like	*z*	in	*zoo*
Д	д	sounds like	*d*	in	*duck*

PRACTICE

00.05 **Listen to the audio first, then complete the activity.**

5 Read the words and connect them with the correct pictures.

те́ннис   сну́кер   стадио́н   кри́кет

(a)

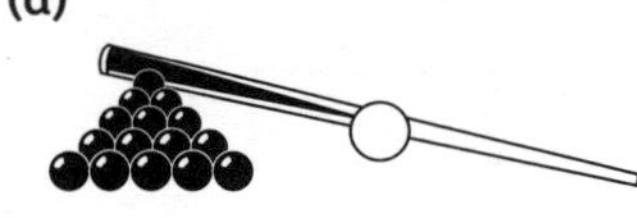

(b)

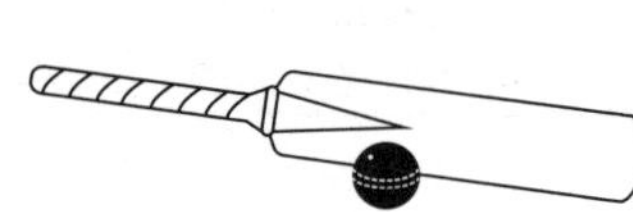

(c)

(d)

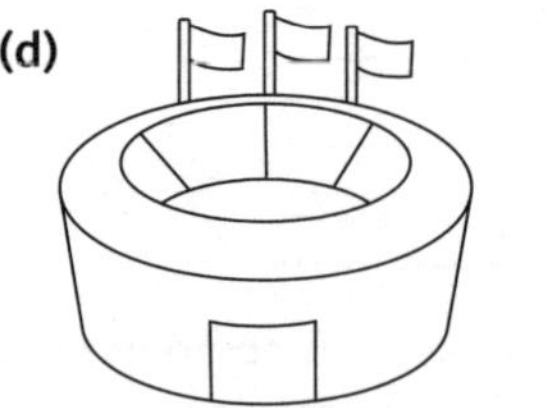

Now match more Russian sports to their English equivalents.

a	старт	**1**	record
b	нока́ут	**2**	knockout
c	тре́нер	**3**	sport
d	реко́рд	**4**	trainer
e	атле́тика	**5**	start
f	спорт	**6**	football
g	футбол	**7**	athletics

6 Connect the Russian and English names of cities around the world.

a	Минск	**1**	Moscow
b	Москва́	**2**	Samarkand
c	Амстерда́м	**3**	Tokyo
d	Ки́ев	**4**	London
e	То́кио	**5**	Madrid
f	Ло́ндон	**6**	Minsk
g	Оде́сса	**7**	Kyiv
h	Мадри́д	**8**	Amsterdam
i	Самарка́нд	**9**	Odesa

7 Match these words about travel and transport with their English equivalents.

a	ви́за	**1**	taxi
b	турист	**2**	passport
c	па́спорт	**3**	tourist
d	такси́	**4**	visa

8 In this grid are nine words which refer to occupations or leisure activities. They are written in capital letters. Read them out loud and pronounce them clearly.

	Д	И	П	Л	О	М	А	Т							
								У			Д				
								Р			О		Т		
							Х	И	М	И	К		Р		
								С			Т		А		
К	О	С	М	О	Н	А	В	Т			О		К		
		Т									Р		Т		
		У											О		
	А	Д	М	И	Н	И	С	Т	Р	А	Т	О	Р		
		Е											И		
		Н											С		
		Т							К	А	П	И	Т	А	Н

Here they are again in lower-case letters. Match them with their English equivalents. In printed form, most Russian capital letters are bigger versions of lower-case letters.

a	диплома́т	**1**	administrator
b	тури́ст	**2**	captain
c	космона́вт	**3**	diplomat
d	хи́мик	**4**	doctor
e	студе́нт	**5**	student (male)
f	администра́тор	**6**	tractor driver
g	до́ктор	**7**	tourist
h	трактори́ст	**8**	cosmonaut
i	капита́н	**9**	chemist

9 Here are ten Russian names, five masculine and five feminine. The feminine names end in -a. Read them all out loud and write the English translations in the blanks provided. Mark the feminine ones.

_______ **Ива́н** _______ **Ни́на** _______ **Алекса́ндр**
_______ **Влади́мир** _______ **Екатери́на**

_______ **Ли́за** _______ **Лев** _______ **Ири́на**
_______ **Валенти́н** _______ **Лари́са**

10 Your next set of words is to do with science. See if you can read them out loud. Don't look at the English equivalents until you finish, then match the English and Russian.

а́том коме́та метео́р кли́мат механи́зм
микроско́п микроб
кило́ литр плане́та луна́ киломе́тр

kilo microscope microbe comet liter atom kilometer
planet mechanism moon meteor climate

11 Match the technical equipment. Cover the English version and pronounce all the words clearly. Underline the Russian for the word that doesn't belong.

a	телеви́зор	**1**	*radio*
b	компью́тер	**2**	*printer*
c	монито́р	**3**	*television*
d	ноутбук	**4**	*computer*
e	лимона́д	**5**	*notebook*
f	ра́дио	**6**	*monitor*
g	при́нтер	**7**	*lemonade*

GROUP 3B: UNFAMILIAR LETTERS WITH FAMILIAR SOUNDS. PART 2.

00.06 Here are three more.

Ф	ф	sounds like	*f*	in	*funny*
Ю	ю	sounds like	*yoo*	in	*universe*
Г	г	sounds like	*g*	in	*good*

PRACTICE

00.07 **Listen to the audio first, then complete the activity.**

12 Here are signs you might see walking around a Russian town. Connect them to their English meanings. To get you started, университéт is *university*.

a stadium
b park
c theater
d ATM
e casino
f kiosk
g zoo
h sauna
i café
j institute
k antiques
l grocer's (**gastronom**)

13 00.08 **Nina is lost. She supports the football team Динáмо (Deenámo) and she is looking for the stadium. Listen to the conversation and repeat it.**

Нúна	Ивáн, где стадиóн?
Ивáн	Стадиóн? Вот стадиóн.
Нúна	А, вот стадиóн. Спасúбо, Ивáн.

When Nina says 'A' it is like saying *Aah* in English.

14 You are visiting Russian friends in their flat (квартúра kvartéera) in a block of flats (дом dom). They mention these domestic objects. Try to read the words out loud first. Then match them with their English equivalents.

лáмпа стул коридóр дивáн
мúксер вáза тóстер туалет лифт

toilet corridor lamp mixer vase toaster
lift sofa (divan) chair

15 Connect these music-related words with their English equivalents.

саксофо́н композѝтор гита́ра пиани́но орке́стр
соли́ст о́пера пиани́ст плейлист хе́ви-метал ро́к

piano opera composer pianist
saxophone playlist orchestra
guitar soloist heavy metal rock

16 You are in a restaurant looking at the menu. Work out what is on the menu then read out the list as if you were giving your order to the server.

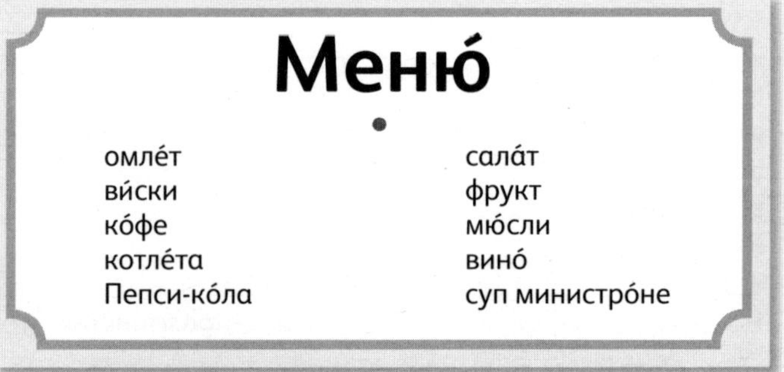

cola muesli salad coffee minestrone soup
whiskey omelette cutlet wine fruit

Congratulations! You can now read 20 letters of the Cyrillic alphabet.

GROUP 3C: UNFAMILIAR LETTERS WITH FAMILIAR SOUNDS. PART 3.

00.09 Here are the last five.

Б	б	sounds like	*b*	in	*bag*
Э	э	sounds like	*e*	in	*leg*
Й	й	sounds like	*y*	in	*toy*
Ё	ё	sounds like	*yo*	in	*yonder*
Я	я	sounds like	*ya*	in	*yak* (except in the syllable before the stress, when it sounds like *yi*)

The letter я on its own means *I*, so this is another word to add to your repertoire! Remember to emphasize each syllable with a stress mark. Wherever ё appears in a word, that syllable will always be stressed.

PRACTICE

00.10 **Listen to the audio first, then complete the activity.**

17 First try matching these cities with their English names.

a Берли́н	**1** Sofia
b Я́лта	**2** Baghdad
c Санкт-Петербу́рг	**3** Berlin
d Софи́я	**4** St Petersburg
e Бухаре́ст	**5** Bucharest
f Багда́д	**6** Yalta

18 All these words are to do with travel and transport. Match the Russian to the correct English word to show that you have understood.

a платфо́рма	**1** airport
b экску́рсия	**2** signal
c авто́бус	**3** express
d трамва́й	**4** Aeroflot ™
e аэропо́рт	**5** platform
f экспре́сс	**6** tram
g сигна́л	**7** excursion
h Аэрофло́т	**8** bus

19 Here is a list of sports vocabulary. Match the correct Russian word to its English equivalent.

a футбо́л	**1** rugby
b волейбо́л	**2** marathon
c бадминто́н	**3** boxing
d марафо́н	**4** volleyball
e а́рмрестлинг	**5** soccer
f бокс	**6** ice hockey
g гимна́стика	**7** basketball
h пинг-по́нг	**8** final
i се́рфинг	**9** surfing
j фина́л	**10** badminton
k ре́гби	**11** ping-pong
l пэйнтбо́л	**12** arm-wrestling
m хокке́й	**13** bodybuilding
n баскетбо́л	**14** gymnastics
o бо́дибилдинг	**15** paintball

20 Try to read these words about music, theater and books out loud then match them with the English versions.

a	симфóния	**1**	bestseller
b	балери́на	**2**	actor (female)
c	поэ́т	**3**	ballet
d	актри́са	**4**	symphony
e	бестсéллер	**5**	ballet dancer
f	актёр	**6**	thriller
g	балéт	**7**	poet
h	три́ллер	**8**	actor (male)

21 You see an online article about science. Can you pronounce and match the following words?

a	энéргия	**1**	kilogram
b	киловáтт	**2**	experiment
c	атмосфéра	**3**	atmosphere
d	килогрáмм	**4**	energy
e	электрóника	**5**	kilowatt
f	эксперимéнт	**6**	electronics

GROUP 4: LETTERS UNLIKE ENGLISH LETTERS

00.11 The first five letters of this group make sounds which will be familiar to you, but in English you would need more than one letter to show the whole sound.

Ж	ж	sounds like	*zh*	in	*pleasure*
Ц	ц	sounds like	*ts*	in	*cats*
Ч	ч	sounds like	*ch*	in	*chicken*
Ш	ш	sounds like	*sh*	in	*ship*
Щ	щ	sounds like	*sch*	in	*borsch*

The last three letters of the group never occur at the beginning of a word. They are:

- ы sounds like *i* in *ill*, but with the tongue further back in the mouth.
- ь is a 'soft sign' which adds a soft *y* sound to the letter before it. Think of the *p* in *pew*. When you see a Russian word written using English letters in this book, a soft sign will be indicated by an apostrophe '. So, for example, the word for computer компьютер will be written kamp'yóoter.
- ъ is a 'hard sign'. This is very rare, and makes a tiny pause between syllables.

Now try reading more words in which any letter of the alphabet may appear! Good luck!

PRACTICE

22 Connect the building signs and the English translations.

a сувени́р b зоомагази́н c полиция

d автошко́ла e *информа́ция* f пи́цца

g банк h проду́кты

1 ______ information 2 ______ souvenirs 3 ______ pet shop

4 ______ pizza 5 ______ driving school 6 ______ groceries

7 ______ police 8 ______ bank

23 Can you guess what these work-related words mean?

a ме́неджер
b конференция
c бри́финг
d ма́ркетинг
e плейлист
f бизнесме́н
g но́у-хау
h бро́кер
i уи́к-энд
j компьютер
k но́утбук

24 Name the members of this family. For example, to answer the first one, you would say: 'Вот ма́ма' out loud and point to the woman in the middle.

ба́бушка кот де́душка ма́ма па́па сын дочь

a Где ма́ма?
b Где сын?
c Где ба́бушка?
d Где па́па?
e Где дочь?
f Где де́душка?
g Где кот?

The children are described in Russian as сын **syn** (*son*) and дочь **doch'** (*daughter*). You could also describe them as брат **brat** (brother) and сестра́ **sistrá** (*sister*).

25 Who are these famous Russians? Put the correct number in the blank.

Writers	**Composers**	**Political leaders**
a _______ Че́хов	**d** _______ Чайко́вский	**g** _______ Ле́нин
b _______ Толсто́й	**e** _______ Рахма́нинов	**h** _______ Горбачёв
c _______ Пу́шкин	**f** _______ Шостако́вич	**i** _______ Е́льцин

Writers:	**1** Pushkin	**2** Tolstoy	**3** Chekhov
Composers:	**1** Rachmaninov	**2** Tchaikovsky	**3** Shostakovich
Political leaders:	**1** Lenin	**2** Yeltsin	**3** Gorbachev

Well done! Now, with every new word, just say each sound in order, emphasizing the stressed syllable, and you should be pronouncing it well enough for a Russian person to understand you.

Part 2: Mechanics of the language

1 *THE* AND *A*

There are no words in Russian for *the* or *a*, so студе́нт means *the student* or *a student*.

2 TO BE

In Russian the verb *to be* is not used to talk about things happening now. *I am a manager* in Russian is simply Я – менеджер (lit. *I manager*). Written Russian may use a dash to replace the verb *to be*: Анто́н – студе́нт *Anton is a student*.

3 GENDER OF NOUNS

A noun is a word that names someone or something. Russian nouns are divided into three groups called gender groups: masculine, feminine and neuter (even non-living things in Russian have a gender). Note that natural gender refers to the biological sex of most animals and people, while grammatical gender refers to certain characteristics of nouns, adjectives, pronouns, verbs and participles. You can tell the gender of a noun simply by looking at the ending. Here are the most common endings.

Masculine

Most masculine nouns end in a consonant or -й. So стадио́н *stadium* and дом *house* or *block of flats* are masculine.

Feminine

Most feminine nouns end in -а or -я. So шко́ла *school*, Оде́сса *Odesa* and эне́ргия *energy* are feminine. (There are exceptions to this rule, e.g. па́па *Dad* which ends in -а but is masculine because of its meaning.)

Neuter

Most neuter nouns end in -о or -е. So метро́ *metro*, вино́ *wine* and кафе́ *café* are all neuter.

Soft sign ь

There is also a small group of nouns ending in a soft sign ь. These may be either masculine or feminine, and you have to learn which gender they are. Кремль *Kremlin* is masculine and меда́ль *medal* and Дочь *daughter* are feminine. Every time you meet a new noun ending in ь, it will have (m) or (f) next to it to show you whether it is masculine or feminine.

To summarize:

Masculine nouns end in	**a consonant**	**парк**
	й	**музе́й**
	ь	**Кремль**
Feminine nouns end in	**а**	**студе́нтка**
	я	**эне́ргия**
	ь	**дочь**
Neuter nouns end in	**о**	**метро́**
	е	**кафе́**

PRACTICE

Read this list of words and put (M) for masculine, (F) for feminine or (N) for neuter in the parentheses to show their gender.

a а́том (_______)
b платфо́рма (_______)
c сала́т (_______)
d пиани́но (_______)
e Аме́рика (_______)
f теа́тр (_______)
g трамва́й (_______)
h информа́ция (_______)
i кино́ (_______)
j дочь (_______)
k волейбо́л (_______)
l вино́ (_______)

Well done! Now you are ready to move on to Unit 1 and real conversations.

1

In this unit, you will learn how to:

» say hello and goodbye.
» greet and address someone.
» say you don't understand.
» ask if someone speaks English.

До́брый день!

My progress tracker

DAY / DATE					
	○	○	○	○	○
	○	○	○	○	○
	○	○	○	○	○
	○	○	○	○	○
	○	○	○	○	○

Russian names

If you have seen a Russian play or read a Russian book in English you probably noticed that Russians appear to have many names. Actually, Russians have three names: their и́мя **éemya** (*first name*); о́тчество **óchistvo** (*'patronymic' name*), formed by their father's first name plus a special ending: -ович **oveech** or -евич **yeveech** for boys and -овна **ovna** or -евна **yevna** for girls; and finally a фами́лия **faméeliya** (*last name* or *surname*). Adults on formal terms may use their first name and patronymic as a mark of respect, adult close friends use first names and children are addressed by their first names. People on first-name terms often use 'diminutive' forms: Еле́на (**Ilyéna**) might be Ле́на (**Lyéna**) for short, Ле́ночка (**Lyénuchka**) or Лену́ся (**Lyino'osya**) affectionately, Лено́к (**Lyinók**) jokingly, Ле́нка (**Lyénka**) perhaps by an angry parent and more rarely but affectionately, Алёна (**Alyóna**) and Алёнушка (**Alyónooshka**).

What are the names of these people's fathers?

1 **Влади́мир Ива́нович Козло́в Vladéemir Eevánovich Kazlóf**

2 **Еле́на Алекса́ндровна Попо́ва Ilyéna Aliksándrovna Papóva**

Vocabulary builder

01.01 **Listen as you look at the words and complete the English translations. Then listen again and try to imitate the speakers.**

GREETINGS

До́брое у́тро.	Dóbroye óotra.	*Good morning.*
До́брый день.	Dóbry dyen'.	**a** _______.
До́брый ве́чер.	Dóbry vyécher.	**b** _______.
Здра́вствуйте.	Zdrástvooeetyi.	*Hello.*
До свида́ния.	Da sveedánya.	*Goodbye.*

NEW EXPRESSIONS

Меня́ зову́т ...	Minyá zavóot ...	*I am called ...*
О́чень прия́тно.	Ochen' preeyátna.	*Pleased to meet you.*
Как вас зову́т?	Kak vas zavóot?	*What's your name?*
Как дела́?	Kak dyilá?	*How are things?*
хорошо́	khurashó	*good/well*
извини́те	eezveenéetye	*Excuse me/I'm sorry*
молодо́й челове́к	maladóy chilavyék	*young man*
вы	vy	*you*
нет	nyet	*no*
я	ya	*I*
не	nye	*not*
де́вушка	dyévushka	*young woman*
да	da	*yes*
Я не понима́ю.	Ya nye paneemáyoo.	*I don't understand.*
Я не зна́ю.	Ya nye znáyoo.	*I don't know.*
Ме́дленнее, пожа́луйста.	Myédlyn-ye-ye, pazháloosta.	*Slower, please.*
Вы говори́те по-англи́йски?	Vy gavaréetye pa-angléesky?	*Do you speak English?*
Я говорю по-ру́сски пло́хо.	Ya gavaryóo pa-róosky plókha.	*I speak Russian badly.*

Диало́ги *Dialogues*

Listen to the conversations and answer the questions. Then listen again and repeat.

ДИАЛОГ 1 *DIALOGUE 1*

01.02 *Some people are greeting each other and saying goodbye at different times of the day.*

1 What time of day is it in each exchange?

Ви́ктор До́брое у́тро, Ната́ша.
Ната́ша До́брое у́тро, Ви́ктор.

Бори́с До́брый день, А́нна.
А́нна До́брый день, Бори́с.

Све́та До́брый ве́чер, Ле́на.
Ле́на До́брый ве́чер, Све́та.

Ири́на Здра́вствуйте!
Анто́н Здра́вствуйте!

Та́ня До свида́ния, И́ва́н.
Ива́н До свида́ния, Та́ня.

2 Find the words in the conversation that mean *good morning, good evening, hello, good day* and *goodbye*.

3 Now cover up the text and see if you can remember how to say:

a good morning
b good evening
c hello
d good day
e goodbye

ДИАЛОГ 2 *DIALOGUE 2*

01.03 *Alison and Igor are having a conversation.*

1 What are Alison and Igor doing?

И́горь	До́брый ве́чер. Меня́ зову́т И́горь.
А́лисон	Очень прия́тно.
И́горь	Как вас зову́т?
А́лисон	Меня́ зову́т А́лисон.
И́горь	Очень прия́тно. Как дела́, А́лисон?
А́лисон	Хорошо́, спаси́бо.

2 How is Alison feeling this evening?

3 Now imagine that you are having the conversation. Say Igor's part, covering up Alison's responses, and vice versa. Then repeat Igor's questions and respond as if you were Alison.

ДИАЛОГ 3 *DIALOGUE 3*

01.04 *Concerning an advert about a flat to rent privately, Valódya has arranged to meet a young man called Sásha and his girlfriend Nástya.*

1 How many people does Valódya approach before he meets Sásha and Nástya?

Воло́дя	Извини́те, молодо́й челове́к, вы Са́ша?
Ми́ша	Нет, я не Са́ша.
Воло́дя	Извини́те ... Де́вушка, вы не На́стя?
Ве́ра	На́стя? Нет, я не На́стя.
Воло́дя	Извини́те, вы Са́ша и На́стя?
Са́ша	Да. Вы Воло́дя?
Воло́дя	Да, я Воло́дя. О́чень прия́тно, Са́ша. О́чень прия́тно, На́стя.

Воло́дя **Valódya** is a diminutive of Влади́мир **Vladéemir**, Са́ша **Sásha** is a diminutive of Алекса́ндр **Aliksándr** and На́стя **Nástya** is a diminutive of Анастаси́я **Anastasíya**.

2 What does Valódya say to get each person's attention?

3 Now listen again and repeat one line at a time.

ДИАЛОГ 4 *DIALOGUE 4*

01.05 *Andrew is having a few problems understanding a new acquaintance at a party.*

1 Why does Andrew say 'oh good'?

Никола́й	Здра́вствуйте.
А́ндрю	Здра́вствуйте.
Никола́й	Как вас зову́т?
А́ндрю	Ме́дленнее, пожа́луйста.
Никола́й	Как вас зову́т?
А́ндрю	Извини́те, я не понима́ю.
Никола́й	Как вас зову́т? Меня́ зову́т Никола́й Петро́вич. Как вас зову́т?
А́ндрю	А, меня́ зову́т А́ндрю. Вы говори́те по-англи́йски?
Никола́й	Да, я говорю́ по-англи́йски.
А́ндрю	*Oh good!* Хорошо́! Я пло́хо понима́ю по-ру́сски.

2 What does Andrew ask Nikalái to do to help him understand the question?

3 Now listen again and repeat one line at a time.

Language discovery

Find suitable words in the dialogues to complete the sentences.

a Извини́те, я _____ понима́ю.

b Вы _____ по-англи́йски?

c Ме́дленнее, _____.

d Я _____ понима́ю по-ру́сски.

There is only one possible answer to sentences **a–c**, but the last sentence could have a choice of answers. Can you explain why?

1 TWO WAYS OF SAYING IT: *YOU* AND *HELLO*

In Russian, as in many languages, there are two words for *you*. English used to have two words – *you* and *thou* – but now we always use *you*. The two Russian words are вы **vy** and ты **ty**. Вы is used when you are speaking to more than one person, or to an adult with whom you are on formal or polite terms. Ты is used when you are speaking informally to one person only. You nearly always use ты to address a child or a close friend or relation. (Let your Russian friends decide whether to use вы or ты with you. It is common to use вы when you meet someone for the first time, and continue to do so until your new acquaintance suggests switching to ты: можно на ты? **mozhno na ty?** *May I use ty?* Your reply should be – **mozhno**. The younger generation often prefer the less formal ты while older people may feel more comfortable using вы even when they have known someone for years.)

There are also two ways of saying *hello*, depending on whether you call someone вы or ты. If you are talking to more than one person or formally to one adult, you say здра́вствуйте **zdrástvooeetyi**, as you have already learned, but if you are talking to a child, close friend or relative, you say здра́вствуй **zdrástvooee**, leaving off the ending.

Your turn!

So, what would you say if you picked up the phone and heard your Russian boss calling? Imagine her name is Валенти́на Ива́новна Valentééna Eevánovna. If, on the other hand, it was your long-lost friend, Ко́ля Kólya, what would you say?

2 ASKING QUESTIONS

01.06 A statement is turned into a question by varying the rise and fall of your voice.

Listen to the examples and repeat.

If you make a statement in Russian, your voice should fall:

Ива́н – студе́нт. **Eeván stoodyént.** *Ivan is a student.*

If you make the statement into a question, your voice should rise:

Ива́н – студе́нт? **Eeván stoodyént?** *Is Ivan a student?*

If the question contains a question word such as *who*, *what*, *where*, *why*, *when* or *how*, your voice should rise on the question word itself:

Как дела́? **Kak dyelá?** *How are things?*

3 TO DO OR NOT TO DO

You have already met people saying that they can and can't do things and probably noticed the little word не **nye** which means *not*. In the last dialogue, Andrew said Я не понима́ю **ya nye paneemáyoo** (*I don't understand*). Никола́й **Nikalái** told him: Я говорю́ по-англи́йски **ya gavaryoó pa-angléesky** (*I speak English*).

Your turn!

1 Give the meaning of these phrases:

- **a** Я зна́ю **ya znáyoo**.
- **b** Я понима́ю **ya paneemáyoo**.
- **c** Я говорю́ **ya gavaryóo**.

If you want to say that you can't do any of these things, simply slip не (*not*) between я and the word which says what you are doing.

2 How do you think you would do that for these sentences?

- **a** I don't know.
- **b** I don't understand.
- **c** I don't speak.

The action words *to know*, *to understand* and *to speak* are verbs. If you want to say that you do any of these things well or badly, slip хорошо́ (*well*) or пло́хо (*badly*) between я and the verb. Look at the examples:

Я хорошо́ зна́ю А́лисон.	**Ya khurashó znáyoo Álison.**	*I know Alison well.*
Я хорошо́ понима́ю А́ндрю.	**Ya khurashó paneemáyoo Ándrew.**	*I understand Andrew well.*
Я пло́хо говорю́ по-ру́сски.	**Ya plókhu gavaryóo pa-róosky.**	*I speak Russian badly.*

By the end of the course you should be able to say truthfully *I speak Russian well*. Why not try it out now! Я хорошо́ говорю́ по-ру́сски! **Ya khurashó gavaryóo pa-róosky!**

4 WHO'S WHO?

You already know how to say я (*I*) and ты or вы (*you*) in Russian. Now you should be ready to learn *he*, *she*, *we* and *they*.

In Russian, *he* is он **on**:

Он – поэ́т.	**On – paét.**	*He is a poet.*

She is similar to *he* but has a feminine ending, она́ **aná**:

Она́ – балери́на.	**Aná – balyiréena.**	*She is a ballet dancer.*

We is мы **my**, rhyming with ты and вы:

Мы – ма́ма и па́па.	**My – máma ee pápa.**	*We are Mum and Dad.*

They is они́ **anée**:

Они́ – Са́ша и На́стя.	**Anée – Sásha ee Nástya.**	*They are Sásha and Nástya.*

Subject pronouns			
я	*I*	**мы**	*we*
ты	*you* (one person, fam.)	**вы**	*you* (more than one person, form.)
он	*he*	**они́**	*they*
она́	*she*		

Practice

1 Fill in a form for a male Russian friend. Match the names with the blanks on the form. Then do the same for a female Russian friend.

a Имя ____________________
b Отчество ____________________
c Фамилия ____________________

1 Влади́мирович
2 Смирно́в
3 Бори́с

d Имя ____________________
e Отчество ____________________
f Фамилия ____________________

4 Ни́на
5 Горбачёва
6 Бори́совна

What is the first name of your male friend's father? And your female friend's father?

2 How would you say hello at these times of day?

a 9.15 **b** 14.45 **c** 20.30

3 Use the letters below to help you complete the responses.

a You meet a Russian person who asks you what your name is.

Mr. X: Как вас зову́т?

You: М ________ з ________ Stuart.

b He says he is pleased to meet you. How does he say that in Russian?

О _______ п _______.

4 You are working in Russia and an old friend and colleague А́нна Миха́йловна calls on you. Choose the correct response.

a Как вас зову́т?

b Я не понима́ю

c Де́вушка

d До свида́ния

e Здра́вствуйте

f Извини́те

5 01.07 **Listen then repeat these words.**

a Здра́вствуйте

b Спаси́бо

c Я говорю́ по-англи́йски

d Хорошо́

e Где Бори́с?

f Я не зна́ю

g Ме́дленнее, пожа́луйста

h Извини́те

6 Match the Russian and English translations.

a Я говорю́ по-англи́йски.	**1** I don't know.
b Я не понима́ю.	**2** I understand Russian well.
c Я хорошо́ понима́ю по-ру́сски.	**3** I speak English.
d Я не зна́ю.	**4** I understand.
e Я понима́ю.	**5** I don't understand.

7 Complete the sentences with one of the words from the box.

До́брый челове́к зову́т не говори́те

a Меня́ ________ Ива́н.

b ________ ве́чер.

c Я ________ понима́ю.

d Вы ________ по-англи́йски?

e Молодо́й ________.

8 Match the questions and answers. Say them out loud.

a Кто он?	**1** Они́ – ба́бушка и де́душка.
b Кто ты?	**2** Она́ – стюарде́сса.
c Кто она́?	**3** Мы – брат и сестра́.
d Кто вы?	**4** Он – студе́нт.
e Кто они́?	**5** Я – космона́вт.

Listen and learn

01.08 Listen and choose the best answers.

1 The speaker says
- **a** good morning.
- **b** good day.
- **c** good evening.

2 The woman is called
- **a** Nina Petrovna.
- **b** Nina Borisovna.
- **c** Anna Petrovna.

3 She
- **a** speaks English.
- **b** doesn't speak English.
- **c** speaks English well.

Test yourself

1 What do these words and phrases mean?
- **a** здра́вствуйте
- **b** до свида́ния
- **c** извини́те
- **d** как вас зову́т?
- **e** вы говори́те по-англи́йски?

2 How would you say these phrases in Russian? Say your answers out loud then check them in the Answer key.
- **a** Say you don't understand.
- **b** Say *you* as if you were talking to a child.
- **c** Say *you* as if you were talking to your boss.
- **d** Say you are pleased to meet someone.
- **e** Ask someone to speak more slowly.

SELF CHECK

	I CAN...
○	... say hello and goodbye.
○	... greet and address someone.
○	... say I don't understand.
○	... ask if someone speaks English.

2

In this unit, you will learn how to:

» name some important places in a town.

» ask and say where things are.

» describe things that you see.

» understand a Russian address.

» count to ten.

Где банк?

My progress tracker

DAY / DATE	🎧	🎤	📖	✏️	💬
	○	○	○	○	○
	○	○	○	○	○
	○	○	○	○	○
	○	○	○	○	○
	○	○	○	○	○

Going places

Passenger transport in Russia includes the автóбус **aftóboos** (*bus*), трамвáй **tramváy** (*tram*), троллéйбус **trallyéiboos** (*trolleybus*) and метрó **mitró** (*underground system*). Generally, you can purchase a талóн **talón** (*ticket*) from a driver or in advance. Other forms of transport include the Маршрýтка **marshróotka** (*minibus taxi*) with a fixed route, and таксú **taksée** (*taxis*) with private drivers ordered via an app for a fixed fare. Russian addresses start with гóрод **górat** (*the city*), then ýлица **óoleetsa** (*the street*), дом **dom** (*the number of the block of flats*), кóрпус **kórpoos** (*the building section number*), then квартúра **kvartéera** (*the flat number*). When writing an адрес **adryes** (*address*), personal names come after the address starting with a family name, followed by the first name and the patronymic name.

Бéлый Byély means *white*. Moscow is often called a White Stone City. Do you know why? Finding this information will help you better understand the history of Moscow.

Vocabulary builder

02.01 Listen as you look at the words, then listen again and try to imitate the speakers.

NEW EXPRESSIONS

москви́ч/москви́чка	maskvéech/maskvéechka	*Moscow resident* (m, f)
Где ...?	Gdye ...?	*Where is ...?*
Э́то	Éto	*It is/Is it?*
вон там	von tam	*over there*
кинотеа́тр	keenotiátr	*cinema*
спра́вочное бюро́	správuchnoye byuró	*information office*
Не́ за что!	Nyé za shto!	*Don't mention it!*
здесь	zdyes'	*here, around here*
он/она́/оно́	on/oná/anó	*it* (m/f/n)
скажи́те	skazhéetye	*tell me*
гости́ница	gastéeneetsa	*hotel*
Како́й э́то го́род?	Kakóy éto górat?	*What sort of city is it?*
како́й/кака́я/како́е	kak-óy/-aya/-óye	*what sort of* (m/f/n)
большо́й/больша́я/большо́е	bal'sh-óy/-aya/-óye	*big* (m/f/n)
краси́вый/краси́вая/краси́вое	kraséev-y/-aya/-oye	*beautiful* (m/f/n)
хоро́ший/хоро́шая/хоро́шее	kharósh-y/-aya/-eye	*good* (m/f/n)
там	tam	*there*
ма́ленький/ма́ленькая/ма́ленькое	mályen'-ky/-aya/-oye	*little* (m/f/n)

Language discovery

Find the three endings for *beautiful* below. Why are they different?

краси́вый го́род **kraséevy górat**

краси́вая кварти́ра **kraséevaya kvartéera**

краси́вое кафе́ **kraséevoye kafé**

Диало́ги *Dialogues*

Listen to the conversations and answer the questions. Then listen again and repeat.

ДИАЛОГ 1 *DIALOGUE 1*

02.02 *Andrew's Russian is getting better every day, and he has gone out to look around Moscow.*

1 What does Andrew need first?

А́ндрю	Извини́те, пожа́луйста, э́то банк?
Москви́чка	Нет, э́то по́чта.
А́ндрю	Где банк?
Москви́чка	Банк вон там.

2 Find the word in the conversation that means *where is?*

3 Now cover up the text and see if you remember how to say *Excuse me***.**

ДИАЛОГ 2 *DIALOGUE 2*

02.03 *Andrew has read online that there's a good film on at the cinema.*

1 Which cinema is he looking for?

А́ндрю	Это кинотеа́тр 'Ко́смос'?
Москви́ч	Нет, э́то кинотеа́тр 'Плане́та'.
А́ндрю	Где кинотеа́тр 'Ко́смос'?
Москви́ч	Извини́те, я не зна́ю.
А́ндрю	Где спра́вочное бюро́?
Москви́ч	Вон там.
А́ндрю	Спаси́бо.
Москви́ч	Не́ за что! До свида́ния.

2 When he can't find the cinema, what does he ask for instead?

3 Without looking at the text, can you remember how to say *thank you***?**

ДИАЛОГ 3 *DIALOGUE 3*

02.04 *Andrew is feeling hungry but can't make up his mind where to eat.*

1 What does he do to help him make up his mind?

Áндрю	Извини́те, где здесь рестора́н?
Москви́ч	Вот он.
Áндрю	Скажи́те, пожа́луйста, где здесь гости́ница?
Москви́ч	Вот она́.
Áндрю	Спаси́бо. Где здесь кафе́?
Москви́ч	Вот оно́.

2 Answer the questions.

a Which three places does he ask about?

b How does he get the man's attention to ask his question?

c Cover up the text and see if you can remember how to say *tell me*.

d Did you notice the three different ways of saying *there it is*?

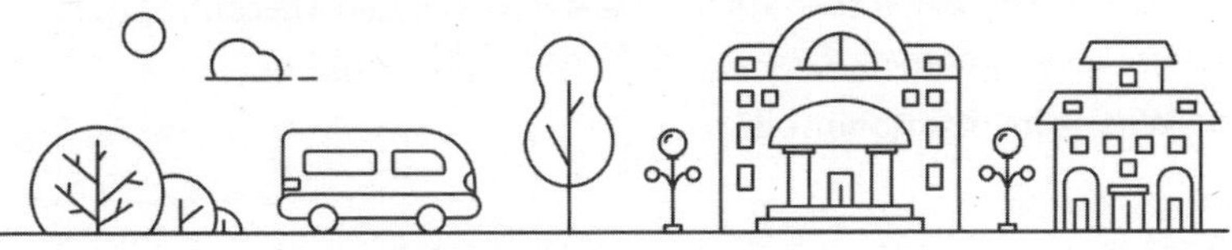

ДИАЛОГ 4 *DIALOGUE 4*

02.05 *While having lunch, he asks a Moscow resident what sort of city Moscow is.*

1 How do you think the Moscow resident feels about his city?

Áндрю	Скажи́те, како́й э́то го́род?
Москви́ч	Это большо́й, краси́вый го́род.

2 Answer the questions.

a Copy what Andrew says and ask in Russian: *What sort of restaurant is it?*

b What does this name mean: Большо́й теа́тр?

c Can you remember how to say *please*?

ДИАЛОГ 5 *DIALOGUE 5*

02.06 *Meanwhile, Valódya asks Sásha and Nástya about the flat in the advert.*

1 Does Sásha paint a positive or negative picture of the flat?

Воло́дя	Скажи́те, кака́я э́то кварти́ра?
Са́ша	Это больша́я, хоро́шая кварти́ра. Там лифт, ванная и краси́вый балко́н.

2 Answer the questions.

a How does Sásha describe the size and quality of the flat?
b What does Sásha tell Valódya about the facilities at the flat?
c How would you say it's a small flat?

ДИАЛОГ 6 *DIALOGUE 6*

02.07 *When Valódya sees the flat, he is disappointed. He complains to Sásha, who contradicts him.*

1 Why is he disappointed?

Воло́дя	Это о́чень маленькая квартира
Са́ша	Нет, э́то не маленькая квартира. Квартира – большая, красивая.

2 The Russian sentences below are in the wrong order. Rearrange them so that they match the conversation in English.

Tourist	Excuse me. Where is the park?
Tour guide	There it is. Over there.
Tourist	What sort of park is it?
Tour guide	It is a beautiful big park.
Tourist	Thank you. Goodbye.

a _______ Како́й э́то парк?
b _______ Спаси́бо. До свида́ния.
c _______ Вот он. Вон там.
d _______ Извини́те. Где парк?
e _______ Это краси́вый, большо́й парк.

Language discovery

02.08 NUMERALS 0–10

1 Listen and repeat.

0	ноль	**nol'**			
1	оди́н	**adéen**	**6**	шесть	**shest'**
2	два	**dva**	**7**	семь	**syem'**
3	три	**tree**	**8**	во́семь	**vósyem'**
4	четы́ре	**chitýrye**	**9**	де́вять	**dyévyat'**
5	пять	**pyat'**	**10**	де́сять	**dyésyat'**

2 Listen again and read the numbers out loud as you listen.

Say the first three numbers without looking, then add three more until you can say them all without looking. Shuffle a pack of playing cards and turn over a card at a time, calling out the number, or throw dice, calling out the score. Do this until you can say the numbers up to ten in random order as soon as you see them.

3 Read these numbers out loud.

пять де́вять четы́ре два шесть ноль

во́семь оди́н де́сять три семь

4 Now try reciting the numbers from 10 down to 0.

1 Э́ТО *THIS IS*

You know that you do not need the verb *to be* in Russian if you are talking about things happening now, as in Анто́н – студе́нт *Anton is a student*, but there is a useful word meaning *this is* or *these are*: э́то. So, э́то телефо́н means *This is a phone*. Э́то is also for questions: Э́то телефо́н? *Is this a phone?*

Э́то рестора́н? Нет, э́то не рестора́н. Э́то кафе́.

2 ОН, ОНÁ, ОНÓ *IT*

In English we use *it* to refer to anything we have already mentioned which is not a person, for example, *it (the bus) is late*. In Russian, every time you want to use *it* you must think whether the noun you are referring to is masculine, feminine or neuter objects.

Look back at the introduction to recall how to tell if a word is masculine, feminine or neuter. You already know that он means *he* and онá means *she*. Он and онá also mean *it* when referring to a masculine and feminine noun respectively. Онó is what you use to refer to a neuter noun.

Notice that the endings of these nouns are the same as the pronouns – он, она, оно. The masculine он ends in a consonant, the feminine онá ends in -а and the neuter онó ends in -о.

Где автóбус?	*Where is the bus?*	Вот он. (m)	*There it is.*
Где вáза?	*Where is the vase?*	Вот онá. (f)	*There it is.*
Где рáдио?	*Where is the radio?*	Вот онó. (n)	*There it is.*

3 КАКÓЙ ЭТО ...? *WHAT SORT OF ...?*

There are also three forms of the word meaning *What sort of ...?* when you are asking about a singular noun. They correspond to masculine, feminine or neuter objects.

Какóй? means *What sort of?* when it refers to a masculine noun.

Какáя? means *What sort of?* when it refers to a feminine noun.

Какóе? means *What sort of?* when it refers to a neuter noun.

Notice that какóй has a masculine ending in -й, какáя has a typical feminine ending in -я and какóе has a typical neuter ending in -е (typical for adjectives).

Какóй э́то суп?	*What sort of soup is it?* (m)
Какáя э́то гитáра?	*What sort of guitar is it?* (f)
Какóе э́то винó?	*What sort of wine is it?* (n)

4 ADJECTIVES

Adjectives and nouns agree with each other in gender and number. So, if you use a singular masculine noun, the adjective describing it will also be singular and masculine. If you want to describe something as *beautiful*, work out which gender the noun is, and use the correct ending to make the adjective agree.

Masculine	**Feminine**	**Neuter**
Это краси́вый парк.	**Это краси́вая ва́за.**	**Это краси́вое ра́дио.**
It's a beautiful park.	*It's a beautiful vase.*	*It's a beautiful radio.*

Look at the other adjectives in your word list. You will notice that the most common endings are -ый (m), -ая (f) and -ое (n). Sometimes, as in ма́ленький, the masculine ending will be spelled -ий because of a spelling rule, which need not concern us here (see Summary of language patterns). Similarly, the neuter form may sometimes be spelled -ее as in хоро́шее. Finally, any masculine adjective with the last syllable stressed will have the ending -о́й as in большо́й.

In your word lists from now on, adjectives will appear in singular masculine form only, unless there is anything unusual about them. Don't worry – even if you get the endings wrong you will still be understood!

Practice

1 Look at the map of part of Moscow. Ask and answer out loud where everything on the map is. Use the following example as a model:

Где здесь парк? Вот он.

LANGUAGE TIP

Note that здесь **zdyes'** means *here*, and used in a question it implies that you do not have a particular park in mind, or do not know if you are looking in the right area, but only want to know where there might be a park around here.

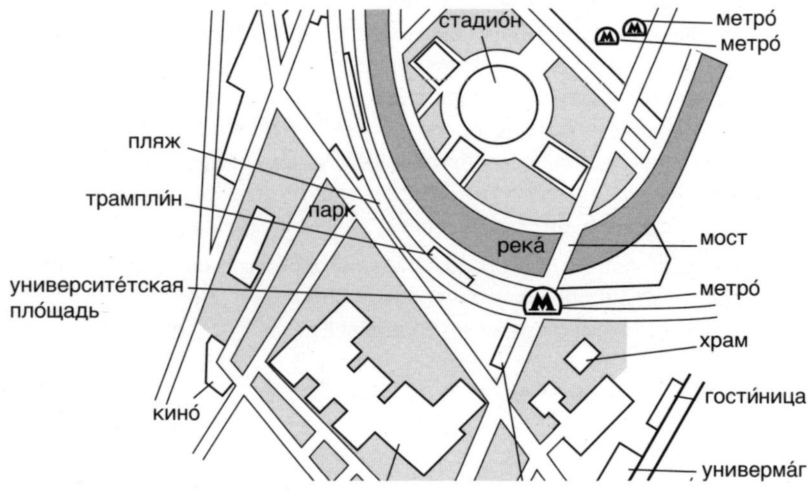

Ключ	Klyooch	Key
река́	**ryiká**	*river*
мост	**most**	*bridge*
стадио́н	**stadeeón**	*stadium*
музе́й	**moozyéy**	*museum*
парк	**park**	*park*
метро́	**mitró**	*metro*
храм	**khram**	*church*
универма́г	**oonivermák**	*department store*
гости́ница	**gastéenitsa**	*hotel*
кино́	**keenó**	*cinema*
университе́т	**ooniversityét**	*university*
трампли́н	**trampléen**	*ski jump*
пляж	**plyash**	*beach*
университе́тская пло́щадь (f)	**ooniversityétskaya plóshshad'**	*university square*

2 Here are signs you might see. Can you figure out the meanings?

a. бульва́р

b. проспе́кт

c. ке́мпинг

d. стоя́нка такси́

e. кафе́-бар

f. тури́стская гости́ница

g. ботани́ческий сад

h. медпу́нкт

i. яхт-клу́б

j. клуб тури́стов

k. кана́л

l. Кра́сная Пло́щадь

m. бассе́йн

n. туристи́ческое аге́нтство

3 Choose the correct answer to each of these questions:

a Где вокза́л? Вот он/она́/оно́.
b Где ста́нция? Вот он/она́/оно́.
c Где трамва́й? Вот он/она́/оно́.
d Где метро́? Вот он/она́/оно́.
e Где шко́ла? Вот он/она́/оно́.
f Где университе́т? Вот он/она́/оно́.
g Где гости́ница? Вот он/она́/оно́.
h Где спра́вочное бюро́? Вот он/она́/оно́.

4 Say these numbers out loud in Russian.

4 5 10 2 8
0 6 1 7 3 9

5 02.09 **Listen to the recording and give the scores of these entirely fictional, amazingly high-scoring international football matches as you hear them. The countries involved are Russia, Italy, Spain, France and England.**

a Металли́ст (Росси́я) ______ Юве́нтус (Ита́лия) ______

b Реа́л (Испа́ния) ______ Дина́мо (Росси́я) ______

c Нант (Фра́нция) ______ Спарта́к (Росси́я) ______

d А́стон Ви́лла (А́нглия) ______ Ла́цио (Ита́лия) ______

e Ньюка́сл Юна́йтед (А́нглия) ______ Атле́тик (Испа́ния) ______

f На́поли (Ита́лия) ______ Торпе́до (Росси́я) ______

6 02.10 **Listen and respond to what the Russian tourist (T) asks you (Y).**

a T: Где спра́вочное бюро́? Y: Say it's over there.

b T: Где тролле́йбус? Y: Say you're sorry, you don't know.

c T: Это библиоте́ка? Y: Say no, it's the post office.

d T: Спаси́бо. Y: Say don't mention it.

7 **Look at these new adjectives, all in masculine form.**

кра́сный	**krásny**	*red*
бе́лый	**byély**	*white*
жёлтый	**zhólty**	*yellow*
зелёный	**zilyóny**	*green*
чёрный	**chórny**	*black*

Below, the same adjectives are in masculine, feminine and neuter forms, and are separated from their nouns. Match the adjectives and nouns.

бе́лая	**вино́**
зелёный	**бана́н**
кра́сное	**табле́тка**
чёрный	**кот**
жёлтый	**сала́т**

Test yourself

1 What do these words and phrases mean?

a Which form of transport is this: троллéйбус?
b What are these three separate numbers: три, пять, дéсять?
c In an address, what does квартúра mean?
d What does this question mean: какóй э́то гóрод?
e What does this mean: э́то крáсное винó?

2 How would you say these words and phrases in Russian? Say your answers out loud then check them in the back of the book.

a six
b two
c Where is the metro?
d Is this a bank?
e Where is the restaurant? There it is.

SELF CHECK

	I CAN . . .
○	. . . name some important places in a town.
○	. . . ask and say where things are.
○	. . . describe things that I see.
○	. . . understand a Russian address.
○	. . . count to ten.

3

In this unit, you will learn how to:

» ask for and give directions.
» ask whether things are available.
» make plural forms.
» say whether somewhere is open or closed.
» count from 10 to 30.

Иди́те пря́мо

My progress tracker

DAY / DATE

At the kiosk

If you need any number of small items, you might ask a stranger on the street как попáсть в киóск **kak papást' v kiósk** (*how to get to a kiosk*). You will find a киóск **kiósk** (*kiosk*) on many city streets in Russia, espcially near a стáнция метрó **stántsiya mitró** (*metro station*). Often kiosks are in the underground passages leading to metro stations or crossing major roads. They sell all manner of goods, including газéты **gazyéty** (*newspapers*), кáрты **kárty** (*maps*) and плáны **plány** (*town plans*), открыы́Ытки **atkrytky** (postcards), сувени́ры **soovinéery** (*souvenirs*), цветы́ **tsvitý** (*flowers*) and конфéты **kanfyéty** (*sweets*).

Look out for the signs: печáть **pichát'** (*newspapers and magazines*) and цветы́ **tsvitý** (*flowers*). Where many kiosks are grouped together they may sell a much wider range of goods, including toys, costume jewelry and clothing.

What do you think you would get if you asked for аплан Москвы́ (plan Maskvý)?

Vocabulary builder

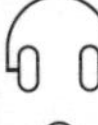

03.01 Listen as you look at the words, then listen again and try to imitate the speakers.

NEW EXPRESSIONS

как попа́сть в ...?	kak papást' v ...?	*How do I/you get to ...?*
центр	tsentr	*the center*
иди́те	eedéetye	*go*
пря́мо	pryáma	*straight ahead*
пото́м	patóm	*then*
нале́во	nalyéva	*to the left*
кра́сный	krásny	*red*
пло́щадь (f)	plóshshad'	*square*
повтори́те	pavtaréetye	*repeat*
Куда́ вы идёте?	Koodá vy eedyótye?	*Where are you going?*
Я иду́ в ...	Ya eedóo v ...	*I'm going to ...*
далеко́	dalyikó	*far, a long way*
недалеко́	nidalyikó	*not far*
напра́во	naprávа	*to the right*
интере́сный	intiryésny	*interesting*
закры́т/а/о	zakrýt/zakrýta/zakrýto	*closed*
на ремо́нт	na rimónt	*for repairs*
Ой, как жаль!	Oy, kak zhal'!	*Oh, what a pity!*
галере́я	galiryéya	*gallery*
откры́т/а/о	atkrýt/atkrýta/atkrýto	*open*
У вас есть ...?	Oo vas yest' ...?	*Do you have ...?*
сувени́р/сувени́ры	soovinéer/soovinéery	*souvenir/s*
конфе́та/конфе́ты	kanfyéta/kanfyéty	*sweet/s*
русский	roosky	*Russian*
америка́нский	amirikánsky	*American*
кни́га/кни́ги	knéega/knéegy	*book/s*
Дом Кни́ги	Dom Knéegy	*bookstore* (literally *House of the Book*)

Диало́ги *Dialogues*

Listen to the conversations and answer the questions. Then listen again and repeat.

ДИАЛО́Г 1 *DIALOGUE 1*

03.02 *Andrew is exploring Moscow. Now he's heading for Red Square and the Kremlin.*

1 Who does he ask for directions?

А́ндрю	извини́те, как попа́сть в центр?
Де́вушка	В центр? Иди́те пря́мо, пото́м нале́во, и там Кра́сная Пло́щадь и Кремль.
А́ндрю	Повтори́те, пожа́луйста.
Де́вушка	Иди́те пря́мо, пото́м нале́во.
А́ндрю	Спаси́бо.

2 Find the words in the conversation that mean *How do I get to …?*

3 Answer true (T) or false (F).

a Andrew asks a female passerby for directions.

b The де́вушка tells Andrew to first go straight ahead, then go to the left.

c Спаси́бо means *goodbye*.

4 Read the conversation line by line and say it out loud.

5 Now imagine that you are having the conversation. Say Andrew's part, covering up the responses, and vice versa. Then repeat Andrew's questions and respond as if you were the other person.

ДИАЛО́Г 2 *DIALOGUE 2*

03.03 *Alison is looking for a place when Igor sees her.*

1 What place is Alison looking for?

И́горь	Здра́вствуйте, А́лисон. Куда́ вы идёте?
А́лисон	Я иду́ в музе́й. Э́то далеко́?
И́горь	Нет, э́то недалеко́. Иди́те пря́мо, и музе́й напра́во. Музе́й о́чень интере́сный.
А́лисон	Спаси́бо. До свида́ния.

2 Email Igor and tell him what Alison is looking for. Igor doesn't know the directions to this place, so give him the directions to give to Alison.

Новое сообщение

Ответить | Ответить всем | Переслать

От:

Кому:

Тема:

Дата:

3 Read the conversation again. Complete the missing information in English.

И́горь ________, А́лисон. Куда́ вы идёте?
А́лисон Я иду́ в ________. ________ далеко́?
И́горь Нет, э́то ________. Иди́те пря́мо, и музе́й напра́во. Музе́й о́чень ________.
А́лисон Спаси́бо. До свида́ния.

4 Now imagine that you are having the conversation. Say Igor's part, covering up Alison's responses, and vice versa. Then repeat Igor's questions and respond as if you were Alison.

ДИАЛОГ 3 *DIALOGUE 3*

03.04 *As Alison sets off, Igor suddenly remembers something.*

1 What does he remember?

И́горь	А́лисон, музе́й закры́т. Закры́т на ремо́нт.
А́лисон	Ой, как жаль!
И́горь	Но галере́я откры́та. И галере́я о́чень интере́сная.
А́лисон	Как попа́сть в галере́ю?
И́горь	Иди́те нале́во, пото́м напра́во, и галере́я пря́мо. Э́то недалеко.

2 Answer true (T) or false (F)

a Igor tells Alison that the museum has an interesting gallery.
b Igor tells Alison to go right then left.
c Ой, как жаль! means *oh, thanks for telling me!*

ДИАЛОГ 4 *DIALOGUE 4*

03.05 *A tourist called Kai is asking a* киоскёр **kioskyór** *(stallholder) about the souvenirs in his kiosk.*

1 What is the stallholder selling?

Кай	У вас есть сувени́ры?
Киоскёр	Да. Вот матрёшки и открытки. Здесь самовар и там русский чай и русское яйцо Фаберже.
Кай	Это бельги́йский шокола́д?
Киоскёр	Нет, ру́сский. О́чень хоро́ший шокола́д.
Кай	А у вас есть кни́ги?
Киоскёр	Нет, иди́те в Дом Кни́ги. Это недалеко́.
Кай	Где Дом Кни́ги?
Киоскёр	Иди́те нале́во, пото́м пря́мо, и Дом Кни́ги напра́во.

2 Where can Kai buy books?

3 What chocolate does the stallholder sell?

Language discovery

03.06 NUMERALS 11–30

1 Listen and repeat.

11 оди́ннадцать	**adéenatsat'**	18 восемна́дцать	**vasyemnátsat'**
12 двена́дцать	**dvyenátsat'**	19 девятна́дцать	**dyevitnátsat'**
13 трина́дцать	**treenátsat'**	20 два́дцать	**dvátsat'**
14 четы́рнадцать	**chitýrnatsat'**	21 два́дцать оди́н	**dvátsat' adéen**
15 пятна́дцать	**pitnátsat'**	22 два́дцать два	**dvátsat' dva**
16 шестна́дцать	**shesnátsat'**	23 два́дцать три	**dvátsat' tree**
17 семна́дцать	**syemnátsat'**	30 три́дцать	**tréetsat'**

2 Now read the numbers as you listen again and repeat.

Numbers 11–19 are made up mostly of the numbers 1–9 plus the ending -надцать, a contracted form of на де́сять (*on ten*). To practice, add 10 or 20 to the numbers on your playing cards or dice, or make up sums:

13 + 8 = 21 трина́дцать плюс во́семь – два́дцать оди́н

30 – 11 = 19 три́дцать ми́нус оди́ннадцать – девятна́дцать

1 КАК ПОПА́СТЬ В ...? *HOW DO I GET TO ...?*

To ask how to get somewhere, simply say Как попа́сть в ... *How to get to ...?* and add the place you want to go. This simple rule works for masculine and neuter nouns, like теа́тр and кафе́. For feminine words, change the noun ending from -а to -у and -я to -ю. (For those people with an interest in grammar, these are accusative endings used after в and на when movement to a place is indicated.)

Masculine	**Feminine**	**Neuter**
Как попа́сть в теа́тр?	Как попа́сть в библиоте́ку? Как попа́сть в галере́ю?	Как попа́сть в кафе́?

Use в when you are going "to" an actual place – when the location you are describing actually exists, such as a city, a village or a building, and use на when you are going "to" a conceptual place – when the location you are describing is a concept, an event or an open space. Как попа́сть на стадио́н? *How do I get to the stadium?* or Как попа́сть на по́чту? *How do I get to the post office?* Note: new words needing на will have (на) next to them in the unit vocabulary list.

2 ГДЕ?/КУДА́? *WHERE?/WHERE TO?*

The word Где? means *Where?* and Куда́? means *Where to?*

Где музе́й?	*Where is the museum?*	Куда́ вы идёте?	*Where are you going to?*

In this unit you met part of the verb *to go*. This refers to going somewhere on foot, not by transport as in я иду́ *I am going*, вы идёте *you are going*.

Your turn

Find the Russian for *Where to* **and** *I am going* **or** *you are going* **in Диало́г 2.**

3 ОТКРЫ́Т/ЗАКРЫ́Т *OPEN/CLOSED*

The endings of these words depend on the gender of the noun each refers to.

Masculine	Feminine	Neuter
Медпу́нкт откры́т.	По́чта откры́та.	Спра́вочное бюро́ откры́то.
Бассе́йн закры́т.	Гости́ница закры́та.	Кафе́ закры́то.

4 PLURAL FORMS OF NOUNS

To make plurals in English we usually add *-s*: *rabbit/rabbits*. in Russian, to make the plural forms of masculine nouns you usually add -ы unless the spelling rule (see Summary of language patterns) makes you use -и instead. For feminine plural forms, remove the last letter (usually -а or -я) and then add -ы or -и. Remember that nouns ending in a soft sign -ь may be either masculine or feminine, and these also lose the last letter before adding -и.

Masculine	Feminine
рестора́н/рестора́ны *restaurant/s*	гости́ница/гости́ницы *hotel/s*
кио́ск/кио́ски *kiosk/s*	библиоте́ка/библиоте́ки *library/libraries*
рубль/рубли́ *rouble/s*	пло́щадь/пло́щади *square/s*

Neuter nouns also lose their last letter before adding -а or -я to make the plural form, so у́тро (*morning*) becomes у́тра. But most neuter nouns you have met so far (бюро́, кака́о, кафе́, кило́, кино́, метро́, пиани́но, ра́дио) do not change form to become plural. Neuter nouns borrowed directly from other languages are exempt from the usual rules.

Practice

1 Read Timur's shopping list and mark where he wants more than one of something (e.g. bananas). The first one has been done for you.

Гастроно́м	**Апте́ка**	**Печа́ть**	**Кио́ск**	**Теа́тр**
бана́ны √	табле́тки	газеты	цветы́	биле́т
ко́фе		и журналы	конфе́ты	
са́хар				
фру́кты				

2 Use one word from each column to make sentences with nouns and adjectives. The first one is done for you.

Example: a И́горь хоро́ший футболи́ст. *Igor is a good footballer.*

a	~~И́горь~~	ру́сская	город
b	Гузе́ль	большо́й	кафе
c	Хард-Рок	краси́вая	газе́та (*newspaper*)
d	Ло́ндон	америка́нское	~~футболи́ст~~
e	Коммерса́нт	~~хоро́ший~~	балери́на

3 Write out three of your sentences. Try not to look back at question 2.

4 Look at the town plan and key on the next page. Say the names of the places then sit down with a Russian person at the café in the left corner and ask if each place is far away.

Q: Гости́ница далеко́? **A: Да, э́то далеко.**

Q: Институ́т далеко́? **A: Нет, э́то недалеко́.**

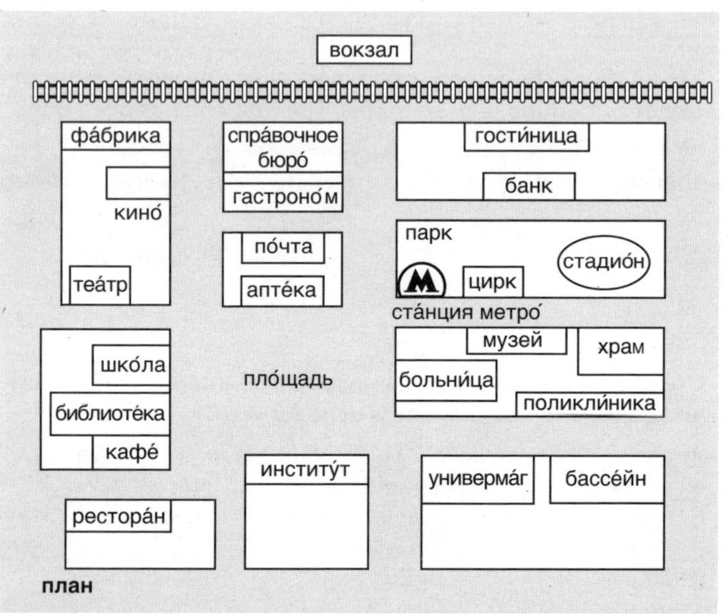

КЛЮЧ KEY

*The English translation is given for new words only.

1 рестора́н; 2 институ́т; 3 универма́г; 4 бассе́йн; 5 кафе́; 6 библиоте́ка; 7 шко́ла; 8 пло́щадь (на); 9 поликли́ника **polykléenika** health center; 10 храм **khram** church; 11 больни́ца **bal'néetsa** hospital; 12 музе́й; 13 теа́тр; 14 апте́ка **aptyéka** pharmacy; 15 цирк; 16 ста́нция метро́ (на) **stántseeya metró** metro station; 17 по́чта (на); 18 парк; 19 стадио́н (на); 20 кино́; 21 гастроно́м; 22 банк; 23 фа́брика (на) **fábreeka** factory; 24 спра́вочное бюро; 25 гости́ница; 26 вокза́л (на) **vakzál** train station

5 Choose the correct form of the question to ask your friend for directions. All the places are feminine, so you will need to change -a to -y and -я to -ю.

Example: Как попа́сть в библиоте́ку? *How do I get to the library?*

a Как попа́сть ... на по́чту?/на по́чта?
b Как попа́сть ... в гости́ница?/в гости́ницу?
c Как попа́сть ... в поликли́ника?/в поликли́нику?
d Как попа́сть ... на фа́брику?/на фа́брика?

6 **Have a conversation with your Russian friend about the places on the town plan. Ask for directions to each place and give replies using идúте напрáво** *go to the right*, **идúте налéво** *go to the left* **and идúте прямо** *go straight ahead*. **Include masculine and neuter places. Remember that masculine and neuter nouns' endings do not change: Как попáсть в ресторáн?** *How do I get to the restaurant?*

7 **Now ask your Russian friend where they are going and give answers.**

Example: Кудá вы идёте? *Where are you going?* Я́ иду́ в гостú ницу *I am going to the hotel.*

8 **03.07 Listen to the conversations and choose the statements which are true.**

a Музéй откры́т.
b Библиотéка закры́та.
c Кафé откры́то.
d Ресторáн закры́т.
e Пóчта откры́та.

9 **Match the questions with suitable answers.**

a У вас есть книги?
b У вас есть кóфе?
c У вас есть таблéтки?
d У вас есть продýкты?
e У вас есть сувенúры?
f У вас есть котлéта и салáт?

1 Нет, идúте в аптéку.
2 Нет, идúте в киóск.
3 Нет, идúте в гастронóм.
4 Нет, идúте в кафé.
5 Нет, идúте в ресторáн.
6 Нет, идúте в библиотéку.

10 **Take a guess. Match the road signs and captions.**

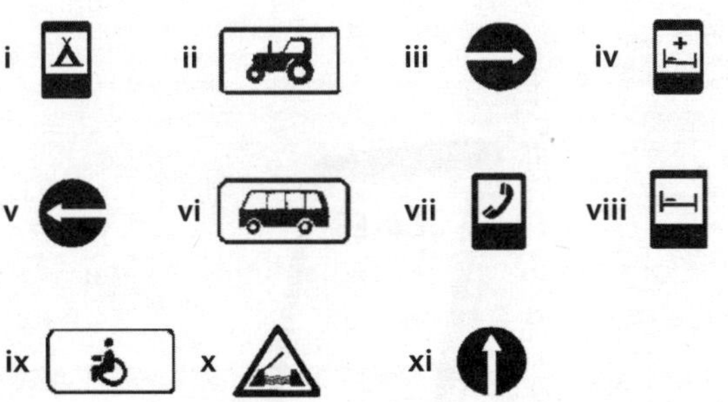

a инвалúды
b движéние прямо
c телефóн
d кéмпинг
e гостúница/мотéль
f больнúца
g автóбусы
h движéние напрáво
i разводнóй мост
j трáкторы
k движéние налéво

11 Match the English with the correct Russian sentence.

a Excuse me, how do I get to the restaurant?
b Go straight ahead, then to the left and the restaurant is on the right.
c Is it far? No, it's not far.
d Is the museum open?
e Do you have any chocolate?

1 Музе́й откры́т?
2 Извини́те, как попа́сть в рестора́н?
3 Э́то далеко́? Нет, э́то недалеко́.
4 У вас есть шокола́д?
5 Иди́те пря́мо, пото́м нале́во, и рестора́н напра́во.

Go further

РАЗГО́ВОР ПО ТЕЛЕФО́НУ *TALKING ON THE PHONE*

You can use your mobile phone in Russia or buy a Russian **sim-kárta** (*SIM card*) and top up your account online or at a **магазин** (*specialist store*). When you get through to a home number, if the person you want does not pick up the phone, ask Руслан до́ма? **Ruslan dóma?** (*Is Ruslan at home?*)

1 You need to call your friend Karina but you have dropped your phone in a puddle. What do you do? Complete each sentence with the correct Russian word/s.

a Find another _______.
b Buy a _______.
c Go to a _______ to top up your account.
d Call the number and ask _______?

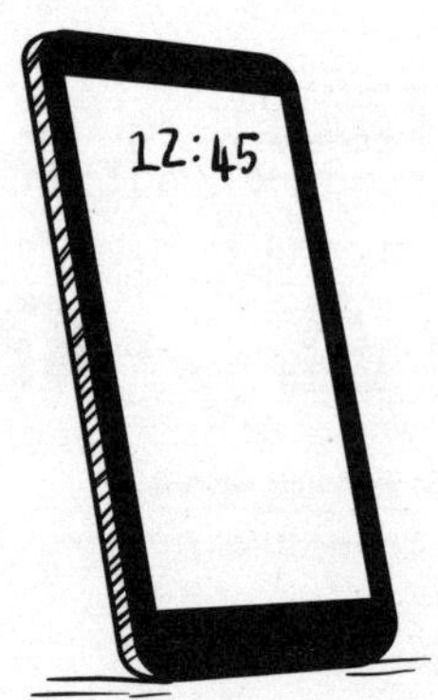

2 03.08 **Listen to each six-digit но́мер телефо́на** (*phone number*) **and complete the missing numbers. The numbers will be read in pairs:**

17 – 25 – 10 семна́дцать – два́дцать пять – де́сять.

a 12 – ______ – 1______

b 25 – ______ – ______7

c 14 – 3______ – ______

d 1______ – ______ – 24

e ______ – ______ – 12

3 Now make up more numbers and read them out clearly.

Test yourself

1 What do these words and phrases mean?

a Как попа́сть в центр?

b У вас есть цветы́?

c Музе́й закры́т.

d Повтори́те, пожа́луйста.

e Это далеко́?

2 How do you say these words and phrases in Russian? Say them out loud, then check the answers in the back of the book.

a 26, 13, 30

b restaurants

c How do I get to the museum?

d Go straight ahead.

e Where are you going to?

SELF CHECK

	I CAN . . .
○	. . . find my way around a Russian town.
○	. . . understand numbers up to 30.
○	. . . understand what закры́т means on a shop door.
○	. . . find out what is available in shops which are open.

R1 Review 1

1 Greet Tamara at the following times of day:

a morning

b afternoon

c evening

Greet Tamara and take your leave:

d Say hello, using the informal version of the word.

e Say goodbye.

Points: ________ /5

2 You ask a passerby to show you where some places are. The passerby says *There it is*. Choose the right word for *it*.

Your question (give the Russian):	The passerby's answer:
a Where is the bank?	Вот он/она́/оно́.
b Where is the hotel?	Вот он/она́/оно́.
c Where is the restaurant?	Вот он/она́/оно́.
d Where is the café?	Вот он/она́/оно́.

Points: ________ /8

3 Complete the missing numbers in each series.

a два, четы́ре, ________, во́семь, ________.

b пять, де́сять, ________, два́дцать, два́дцать пять, ________.

c оди́н, три, пять, семь, де́вять, ________, ________, пятна́дцать, ________, девятна́дцать.

Points: ________ /7

4 What questions would you ask to get these replies?

a Музей откры́т.

b Нет, э́то недалеко́.

c Я иду́ в парк.

d Да, вот хоро́ший ру́сский шокола́д.

e Иди́те нале́во, и Большо́й Теа́тр напра́во.

Points: ________ /5

5 Ask in Russian how to get to these places. Pay attention to the endings of the words.

a library
b swimming pool
c café
d stadium

Points: _______ /4

6 Complete the table. Choose the correct adjective endings and give translations.

Adjective	Noun	English translation (adj-noun)
a интере́сный/ая/ое	кни́га	
b кра́сный/ая/ое	авто́бус	
c ма́ленький/ая/ое	кафе́	

Points: _______ /6

Total points: _______ /35

In this unit, you will learn how to:

» say what you want.
» pay for something in a shop.
» say that something belongs to you.
» make plural forms of adjectives.
» count from 30 to 100.

Что вы хоти́те?

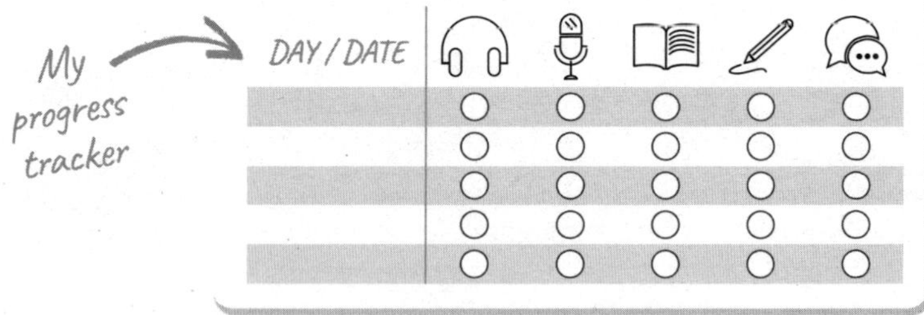

Shopping in Russia

Where to go? You might enjoy a spending spree at a modern торго́вый центр **torgóvy tsentr** (*shopping center*) or at a **универмаг oonívermak** (*department store*) such as ГУМ or Гла́вный универса́льный магази́н (*GUM Main Department Store*) in Red Square in Moscow, Russia's most famous. For food, try one of the grocery stores or a ры́нок **rýnok** (*market*). For о́вощи и фру́кты **óvashshee ee fróókty** (*fresh vegetables and fruit*), молоко́ **mulakó** (*milk and dairy produce*) and мя́со и ры́ба **myása ee rýba** (*meat and fish*), the local markets are good. While shopping you might take a break at a кафе́ **kaféh** (*café*). To attract attention, you can use a gesture of a raised hand, as well as a nod of the head to invite the server. Use the server's name, displayed on their name tag, to address them.

What do you think these shops are: су́пермаркет and ги́пермаркет?

Vocabulary builder

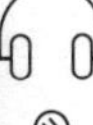

04.01 Listen as you look at the words, then listen again and try to imitate the speakers.

NEW EXPRESSIONS

что?	shto?	*What?*
Что вы хоти́те купи́ть?	Shto vy khatéetye koopéet'?	*What do you want to buy?*
пода́рок/пода́рки	padárak/padárky	*present/s*
я хочу́	ya khachóo	*I want*
балала́йка	balaláika	*balalaika*
пойдём	paeedyóm	*let's go*
покажи́те	pukazhéetye	*show (me)*
Ско́лько сто́ит?	Skól'ka stóeet?	*How much is it?*
сто пятьдеся́т рубле́й	sto pidisyát rooblyéi	*150 roubles*
Где плати́ть?	Gdye platéet?	*Where do I pay?*
фрукто́вый сок	frooktóvy sok	*fruit juice*
и́ли	éely	*or*
иди́те сюда́	eedéetye syoodá	*come here*
Что у вас есть?	Shto oo vas yest'?	*What have you got?*
минера́льная вода́	minirál'naya vadá	*mineral water*
с	s	*with*
с лимо́ном	s leemónum	*with lemon*
с са́харом	s sákharum	*with sugar*
с молоко́м	s mulakóm	*with milk*
сейча́с	seychás	*now, right away*
ваш/ва́ша/ва́ше/ ва́ши	vash/vásha/váshe/váshy	*your* (m/f/n/pl)
мой/моя́/моё/мой	moy/mayá/mayó/mayée	*my* (m/f/n/pl)
джаз	dzhaz	*jazz*

1 Look at what the customers say in a café. What do they want?

a Ната́ша, чай с лимоном, пожалуйста!

b Па́вел, ко́фе с моло́ко́м, пожалуйста!

Диало́ги *Dialogues*

Listen to the conversations and answer the questions. Then listen again and repeat.

ДИАЛО́Г 1 *DIALOGUE 1*

04.02 *Peter is visiting Russia on business but before returning home he goes shopping with a colleague, Sofia Ivanova.*

1 What sort of shopping does Peter want to do?

Со́фия Ивано́ва	Что вы хоти́те купи́ть, Пи́тер?
Пи́тер	Сувени́ры и пода́рки.
Со́фия Ивано́ва	Каки́е сувени́ры и пода́рки?
Пи́тер	Я хочу́ купи́ть кни́ги, матрёшки, шокола́д, во́дку и балала́йку.
Со́фия Ивано́ва	Хорошо́. Пойдём в Дом Кни́ги.

ДИАЛО́Г 2 *DIALOGUE 2*

04.03 *In Дом Кни́ги Dom Knéegy (the bookshop) Peter soon gets into his stride.*

1 Does Peter decide to buy the first item he asks for?

Пи́тер	У вас есть кни́га 'А́нна Каре́нина'?
Молодо́й челове́к	Да.
Пи́тер	Покажи́те, пожа́луйста.
Молодо́й челове́к	Вот она́.
Пи́тер	Ско́лько сто́ит?
Молодо́й человек	пятьсот пятьдеся́т рубле́й.
Пи́тер	Где плати́ть?
Молодо́й челове́к	Иди́те в ка́ссу.
Пи́тер	Спаси́бо.

2 Answer the questions about Dialogue 1.

- **a** What two categories of items does Peter want to buy?
- **b** What item(s) does Peter want to buy more than one of?
- **c** Does Sofia Ivanova think Peter's list is a good one?
- **d** Where does Sofia Ivanova suggest they start?

3 Do the following for Dialogue 2.

- **a** Answer yes or no: Is there a ка́сса in this shop?
- **b** Find the item Peter asks for. How much does it cost?

4 If the young man behind the counter had given the price as пятьсот двена́дцать рубле́й, how much would this have been?

ДИАЛО́Г 3 *DIALOGUE 3*

04.04 *Peter and Sofia Ivanova are tired from their shopping.*

1 Where do they go next?

Со́фия Ивано́ва	Что вы хоти́те, Пи́тер?
Пи́тер	Я хочу́ фрукто́вый сок и́ли чай, пожа́луйста.
Со́фия Ивано́ва	Извините, пожа́луйста. У вас есть фрукто́вый сок?
Официа́нтка	Извини́те, нет.
Со́фия Ивано́ва	Что у вас есть?
Официа́нтка	Чай, ко́фе, минера́льная вода́, пепси-ко́ла.
Пи́тер	Да́йте, пожа́луйста, чай с лимо́ном и с са́харом.
Со́фия Ивано́ва	И ко́фе с молоко́м.
Официа́нтка	Чай с лимо́ном и с са́харом, и ко́фе с молоко́м. Сейча́с.

2 Answer the questions.

- **a** Peter says he wants a choice of two drinks. Which ones are they?
- **b** Which cold drinks does the server suggest?
- **c** What do Peter and Sofia Ivanova decide to drink?

ДИАЛÓГ 4 *DIALOGUE 4*

04.05 *While they wait, Peter and Sofia Ivanova look at Peter's purchases. Sofia Ivanova speaks some English, but they agreed to speak only Russian in the morning and English in the afternoon.*

1 What does Sofia Ivanova ask Peter?

Сóфия Иванóва	Что у вас есть?
Пи́тер	Вот кни́га 'А́нна Карéнина' и матрёшки.
Сóфия Иванóва	Как хорошó. Э́то óчень краси́вые матрёшки. Пи́тер, э́то ваш журнал?
Пи́тер	Да, э́то мой журнал 'Ру́сский джаз'.
Сóфия Иванóва	И вот мой журнал. 'Русская опера'.
Официáнтка	Вот чай и кóфе.
Пи́тер	Спаси́бо.
Сóфия Иванóва	*Oh look, it's twelve o'clock. We can speak English now!*

2 What did Peter buy in addition to books and dolls?

3 What does Sofia Ivanova say about the dolls Peter has bought?

4 Now go back and listen to all the conversations again.

The first language skills a child picks up come from listening. Speaking and reading come later. Listen to Russian whenever you can. Even if you don't understand, you will get used to the sounds and learn how to imitate them.

5 Peter has received an email from a friend with a list of great Russian writers. Read the list out loud, starting with the author of *Ánna Karénina*.

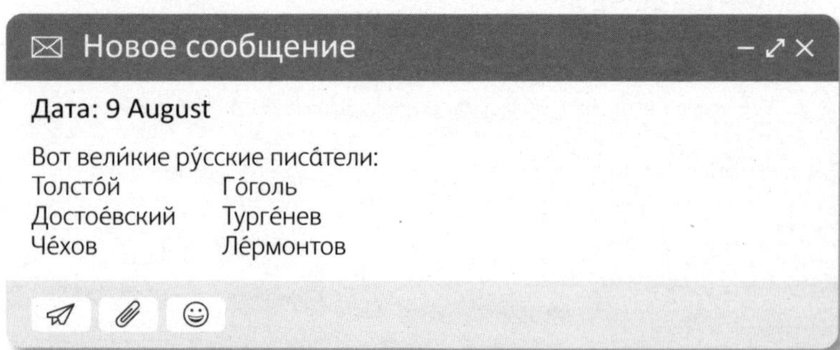

Новое сообщение

Дата: 9 August

Вот вели́кие ру́сские писáтели:

Толстóй	Гóголь
Достоéвский	Тургéнев
Чéхов	Лéрмонтов

Language discovery

1 PLURAL ADJECTIVES

In English, the adjective form is the same for one or several items: *big blue balloon, big blue balloons*. In Russian, remember there are three forms of singular adjectives to match the singular nouns: masculine, feminine and neuter (see Unit 2). Now that you know how to form plural nouns (e.g. конфéты *sweets*), you can use adjectives with them easily as the gender of the plural noun you refer to doesn't matter. There is only one type of plural adjective ending: -ые. This may also be written -ие if the spelling rule applies (see Summary of language patterns).

краси́вые кни́ги *beautiful books*

хоро́шие конфéты *good sweets*

больши́е пи́ццы *big pizzas*

The same ending is used with the plural form каки́е ...? *what sort of ...?*

Каки́е сувени́ры и пода́рки? *What sort of souvenirs and presents?*

2 MY PIZZA AND YOUR PIZZA

There are also different gender forms of the words *my* and *your*.

Masculine	Feminine	Neuter	Plural
мой па́спорт	**моя́** пицца	**моё** пиани́но	**мои́** цветы́
my passport	*my pizza*	*my piano*	*my flowers*
ваш па́спорт	**ва́ша** пицца	**ва́ше** пиани́но	**ва́ши** цветы́
your passport	*your pizza*	*your piano*	*your flowers*

These words also use the typical endings: -й and the consonant -ш for masculine forms, -я and -а for feminine forms, -ё and -е for neuter forms and -и for plurals.

3 I WANT TO BUY A MATRYOSHKA

Did you notice what happens to the endings of the feminine nouns in Диало́г 1? Peter says: Я хочу́ купи́ть кни́ги, матрёшки, шокола́д, во́дку и балала́йку. Во́дка and балала́йка have changed to во́дку and балала́йку.

Once again, this is the accusative form. It occurs when a feminine noun is the person or thing with something done to it, or, in grammatical terms, is the direct object of a verb: a noun that answers the question *what?* asked after the verb.

Here are some examples of direct objects in English:

She baked bread.	She baked what?	Bread.
He likes opera, books, wine.	He likes what?	Opera, books, wine.
He eats pizza.	He eats what?	Pizza.

And in Russian:

Я хочу́ купи́ть матрёшку.	You want to buy what?	А матрёшка.
Я хочу пепси-ко́лу.	You want what?	Cola.

4 IMPERATIVES: DO THIS, DO THAT!

Did you realize that you can already give people eight different orders or requests in Russian? The first you learned was Здра́вствуйте (*hello*) (lit., *Be healthy!*)

Others which you know are:

извини́те	*excuse (me)*	покажи́те	*show (me)*	повтори́те	*repeat*
напиши́те	*write*	да́йте	*give (me)*	скажи́те	*tell (me)*
иди́те	*go*				

Add пожа́луйста to be polite, and you should be able to get things done!

Practice

1 Choose a question word from the box to complete these dialogues.

Как Что Где Кто Куда́

a Q: ________ теа́тр? A: Вот он.
b Q: ________ вас зову́т? A: Меня́ зову́т Ни́на.
c Q: ________ вы идёте? A: Я иду́ на по́чту.
d Q: ________ вы хоти́те? A: Я хочу́ суп, хлеб и во́дку.
e Q: ________ э́то? A: Это Са́ша. Он – мой сын.

2 You work in a Russian kiosk. You cannot keep everything on display, but you have a list so that you know what is tucked away in boxes.

a Study your inventory so you know what you have.

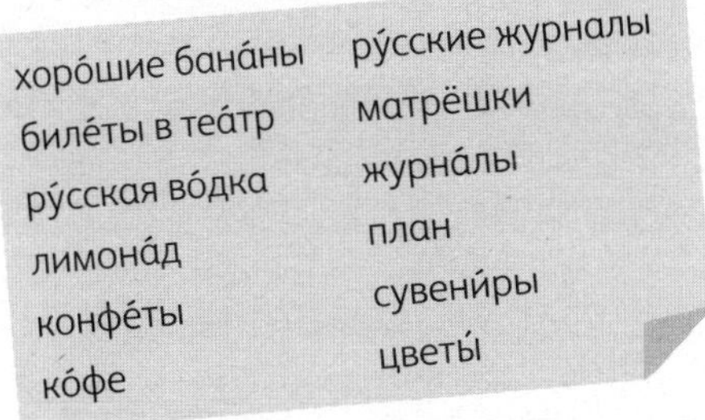

b A tourist comes up and asks if you have varius items. Use the prompts to complete the conversation below. If you have the items, tell them all about them. If not, say извини́те, нет. Look at the example.

Example: Tourist У вас есть сувени́ры?

You: Да, есть. Вот краси́вые ру́сские матрёшки.

1 Tourist: У вас есть самова́р?

You ____________________

2 Tourist У вас есть журна́лы? Каки́е? Ру́сские и́ли америка́нские?

You ____________________

3 Tourist У вас есть бана́ны?

You ____________________

c Now carry on the conversation. You could ask if the tourist wants any sweets, or they could ask you how much something costs.

3 Give the correct orders or requests for each situation.

a repeat ____________

b show (me) ____________

c give (me) ____________

d go ____________

e tell (me) ____________

f write ____________

g excuse me ____________

4 You are in a possessive mood. Every time Artem claims that an item belongs to him, you say it is yours. Look at the example; then for *my*, choose ой/оя́/оё/ои́ and for *your*, choose аш/а́ша/а́ше/а́ши to complete the sentences.

Example: Бори́с Э́то мой микроско́п.

Вы Нет, э́то не ваш микроско́п. Э́то мой микроско́п.

a Бори́с Э́то моё ра́дио.

Вы Нет, э́то не в________ ра́дио. Э́то м________ ра́дио.

b Бори́с Э́то моя́ кни́га.

Вы Нет, э́то не в________ кни́га. Э́то м________ кни́га.

c Бори́с Э́то мои́ гита́ры.

Вы Нет, э́то не в________ гита́ры. Э́то м________ гита́ры.

d Бори́с Э́то мой биле́т.

Вы Нет, э́то не в________ биле́т. Э́то м________ биле́т.

5 04.06 Listen to find out what people want. Choose the correct items from the list as you hear them. Then listen again and mark each feminine item. These will have changed their endings from -а to -у and -я to -ю. Look up any words you do not know.

a ________ вино́ ________ конфе́ты ________ чай с лимо́ном

b ________ во́дка ________ пи́цца ________ ко́фе с са́харом

c ________ суп ________ смета́на ________ омле́т

d ________ борщ ________ фру́кты ________ пепси-ко́ла

6 Match the adjectives and nouns.

a большо́й	**1** сад
b ма́ленькое	**2** конфе́ты
c краси́вые	**3** челове́к
d ру́сские	**4** вино́
e интере́сная	**5** журна́лы
f молодо́й	**6** теа́тр
g ботани́ческий	**7** кни́га
h хоро́шие	**8** ра́дио
i бе́лое	**9** цветы́

7 There are many situations you could now handle if you were visiting Russia. Look at the pictures and answer these questions to make sure.

a Что вы хоти́те?

b Куда́ вы идёте?

c Что э́то?

d Метро́ закры́то?

e Э́то ваш биле́т? (Yes.)

a

b

c

d

e

Go further

MONEY AND NUMBERS

04.07 Numerals 10–100

Listen as you read the numbers then listen again and repeat.

10	де́сять	**dyésyat'**	70	се́мьдесят	**sémdyesyat**
20	два́дцать	**dvátsat'**	80	во́семьдесят	**vósyemdyesyat**
30	три́дцать	**tréetsat'**	90	девяно́сто	**dyevinósta**
40	со́рок	**sórak**	100	сто	**sto**
50	пятьдеся́т	**pidisyát**	146	сто со́рок шесть	**sto sórak shest'**
60	шестьдеся́т	**shesdisyát**			

If you are visiting Russia, you will need to learn relatively high numbers to cope with the prices in roubles. Here is a 1,000-rouble note.

A *rouble* is рубль in Russian, and you may hear it as: рубль, рубля́, рубле́й. If you do not recognize the number with it, ask the salesperson to write down the price for you: Напиши́те, пожа́луйста **napeeshéetye, pazháloosta** (*write, please*).

Try it!

Use this grid to work on your numbers. Cover up all but one line, and read out the ones you see. Try it again in a day or two, and see if you are any quicker.

1	14	36	97	12
8	122	3	88	45
64	199	20	17	150
7	13	65	10	63
144	21	19	5	111

PRACTICE, PRACTICE!

Every time you see a number in your daily life, say it in Russian, as long as it doesn't distract you from driving or working!

Test yourself

1 What do these words and phrases mean?

a Что вы хоти́те купи́ть?

____

b Что у вас есть?

____

c Покажи́те, пожа́луйста.

____

d Ско́лько сто́ит?

____

e Да́йте, пожа́луйста, ко́фе.

____

2 How would you say these words and phrases in Russian? Say your answers out loud then check them in the back of the book.

a tea with lemon
b 120
c my passport
d repeat, please
e excuse me

SELF CHECK

	I CAN . . .
○	. . . say what I want.
○	. . . pay for things in a shop.
○	. . . say who things belong to.
○	. . . talk about plural pizza or pizzas.
○	. . . count from 30 to 100.

In this unit, you will learn how to:

» give your details when booking into a hotel.
» say the letters of the alphabet and fill in a form.
» say what nationality you are and what you do.
» say where you work.
» specify 'this' or 'that'.
» count from 100 to 1,000.

В гости́нице

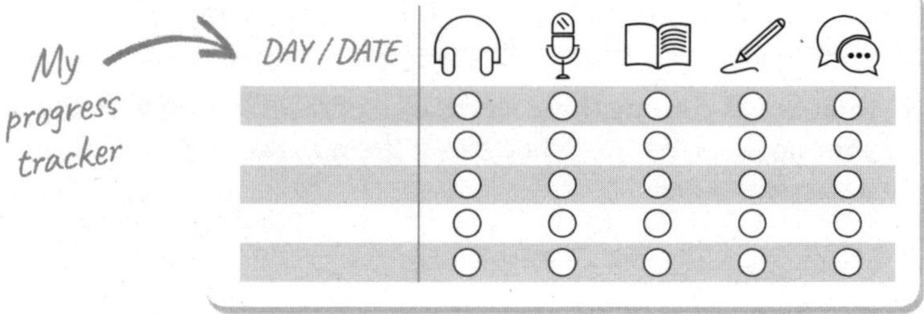

Hotel accommodation

If you are traveling to Russia, you will need a туристи́ческая ви́за **tooreestéecheskaya véeza** (*tourist visa*) or би́знес ви́за **béeznes véeza** (*business visa*). Accommodation options range from a кварти́ра **посуточно kvartéera pasóotochno** (*apartment available on a per night basis*), to a оте́ль **atyél'**/гости́ница **gastéenitsa** (*hotel/inn*), a хо́стел **hóstyel** (*hostel*) or апарт-отель **apart-atyel'** (*apart-hotel*). In a hotel, you may meet the администра́тор **admineestrátor** (*administrator*) at the ресе́пшн **risépshn** (*reception desk*) when you arrive. Most hotels are wheelchair accessible with a пандус **pándus** (*ramp*) or лифт **lift** (*elevator*). When checking in with your name and address, you may be asked Как э́то пи́шется? **Kak éto péeshetsa?** (*How is that written?*)

If you are going on holiday to Russia, where would you stay?

a **би́знес ви́за** **b** **администра́тор** **c** **оте́ль**

Vocabulary builder

05.01 **Listen as you look at the words, then listen again and try to imitate the speakers.**

AT THE HOTEL

Одну́ мину́точку.	Adnóo minóotuchkoo.	*(Wait) one moment.*
Слу́шаю вас.	Slóoshayoo vas.	*I'm listening to you.*
ко́мната	kómnata	*room*
но́мер	nómyer	*hotel room/number*
Запо́лните э́тот бланк.	Zapólneetye étot blank.	*Fill in this form.*
Мо́жно?	Mózhna?	*Is it possible/Would you mind?*
Кто вы по профе́ссии?	Kto vy pa prafyéssee?	*What do you do?*
гражда́нство	grazhdánstva	*nationality/citizenship*
бага́ж	bagásh	*luggage*
чемода́н	chimadán	*suitcase*
ключ	klyooch	*key*

NEW EXPRESSIONS

так	tak	*so*
но	no	*but*
я пишу́	ya peeshóo	*I write.*
А́нглия	Ángleeya	*England*
учи́тельница/учи́тель	oochéetyelneetsa/ oochéetyel'	*teacher* (f/m)
я рабо́таю	ya rabótayoo	*I work.*
в	v	*in*
шко́ла	shkóla	*school*
англича́нка	angleechánka	*English woman*
су́мка	sóomka	*bag*
аккордео́н	akordeón	*accordion*
душ	doosh	*shower*
ва́нная	vánnaya	*bathroom*
туале́т	tooalyét	*toilet*
буфе́т	boofyét	*snack bar*
внизу́	vneezóo	*downstairs*

Диало́ги *Dialogues*

Listen to the conversations and answer the questions. Then listen again and repeat.

ДИАЛО́Г 1 *DIALOGUE 1*

05.02 *Fiona arrives at a hotel in Minsk, Belarus, where she's reserved a room.*

1 What is the first question she has to fill in on the form?

Фио́на Здра́вствуйте.

Администра́тор Одну́ мину́точку. Да, слу́шаю вас.

Фио́на Меня́ зову́т Фио́на Ха́рисон. Я хочу́ ко́мнату, пожа́луйста.

Администра́тор (*looks through bookings*) Фио́на Ха́рисон? Да, вот ва́ша фами́лия. Ва́ша ко́мната но́мер 38 (три́дцать во́семь).

Фио́на Спаси́бо.

Администра́тор Запо́лните э́тот бланк.

Фио́на (*handing the form to the administrator for help*) Мо́жно, пожа́луйста? Я говорю́ по-ру́сски, но пло́хо пишу́.

Администра́тор Мо́жно. Как ва́ша фами́лия?

Фио́на Фами́лия Ха́рисон, и и́мя Фио́на.

Администра́тор Так, Ха́рисон. Как э́то пи́шется, Фио́на?

Фио́на Ф – и – о – н – а.

Администра́тор Како́й у вас а́дрес?

Фио́на А́нглия, Ше́лтон, Улица Кро́сли, дом 13 (трина́дцать).

Администра́тор И кто вы по профе́ссии?

Фио́на Я учи́тельница. Я рабо́таю в шко́ле в Ше́лтоне.

Администра́тор Како́е у вас гражда́нство?

Фио́на Я англича́нка.

Администра́тор Ваш па́спорт, пожа́луйста.

Фио́на Вот он.

Администра́тор Спаси́бо. У вас есть бага́ж?

Фио́на Да, вот мой чемода́н, моя́ су́мка и мой аккордео́н.

Администра́тор Вот ваш ключ.

2 **What are the other questions Fiona has to answer? Find them in the conversation and put them here:**

a ____________________

b ____________________

c ____________________

d ____________________

3 **Which document does she have to present?**

4 **What items of luggage does she have?**

5 **What is Fiona's но́мер?**

ДИАЛО́Г 2 *DIALOGUE 2*

05.03 *Fiona is shown to her room.*

1 **What facilities does Fiona's room have?**

Администра́тор	Вот ва́ша ко́мната. Вот у вас телеви́зор, телефо́н и балко́н. В номере душ, ва́нная и туале́т.
Фио́на	Спаси́бо. Скажи́те, в гости́нице есть рестора́н?
Администра́тор	Да, рестора́н, буфе́т и бар. Но рестора́н сейча́с закры́т.
Фио́на	Как жаль! Как попа́сть в буфе́т?
Администра́тор	Буфе́т напра́во. Э́то недалеко́.
Фио́на	И бар?
Администра́тор	Бар внизу́.

2 **What does Fiona ask about the hotel facilities? Which facility is closed?**

3 **Where is she directed?**

4 **Ask the Администра́тор about the facilities of your hotel in Moscow. Put your questions here:**

a ____________________

____

b ____________________

____

c ____________________

____

05.04 Learn some words for introductions before going to the conversation! Listen as you read, then listen again and repeat.

Где вы живёте?	**Gdye vy zheevyótye?**	*Where do you live?*
Где вы рабо́таете?	**Gdye vy rabótayetye?**	*Where do you work?*
Инжене́р	**eenzhinyér**	*engineer*
Кени́ец	**kenééyets**	*Kenyan*
Францу́женка	**frantsoozhenka**	*French woman.*
я живу́	**ya zheevóó**	*I live.*
продаве́ц/ продавщи́ца	**pradavyéts/ pradavshshéetsa**	*shop assistant* (m/f)
коне́чно	**kanyéshna**	*of course*
ру́сский/ру́сская	**róóskee/róóskaya**	*Russian man/woman*
америка́нец	**amyirikányets**	*American man.*
врач	**vrach**	*doctor*
испа́нка	**eespánka**	*Spanish woman.*

ДИАЛО́Г 3 *DIALOGUE 3*

05.05 *Fiona has come to Minsk for an international conference of accordion players. At their first meeting, Fiona gets the ball rolling.*

1 What does Fiona ask everyone to do?

Фио́на	Кто вы по профе́ссии? Где вы живёте и где вы рабо́таете?
Джомо	Меня́ зову́т Джомо. Я инжене́р. Я рабо́таю в институ́те в Найроби. Я кениец.
Брижи́т	Здра́вствуйте, меня́ зову́т Брижи́т. Я францу́женка. Я учи́тельница и я живу́ в Лио́не. Я там рабо́таю в шко́ле.
Серге́й	Меня́ зову́т Серге́й. Я продаве́ц и я рабо́таю в магази́не здесь в Минске. Я белорус.
Грег	Здра́вствуйте, я америка́нец и меня́ зову́т Грег. Я актёр и я живу́ в Нью Йо́рке.
Ири́на	Я врач. Меня́ зову́т Ири́на. Я рабо́таю в поликли́нике в Но́вгороде. Я ру́сская.
Хуани́та	Меня́ зову́т Хуани́та. Я продавщи́ца и рабо́таю в магази́не. Я живу́ в Барсело́не. Я испа́нка.

Language discovery

What is happening to the end of the last word in each phrase and why?

Как попа́сть в Но́вгород?	**but**	**Я рабо́таю в Но́вгороде.**
Как попа́сть в Барсело́ну?	**but**	**Я живу́ в Барсело́не.**
Я иду́ в шко́лу.	**but**	**Я рабо́таю в школе.**

1 HOW TO SAY *IN*

When в and на mean *in* or *at* a certain place (vs. *to* a place), they trigger the prepositional case in the word that comes after. You use в unless you see (на) next to the word in your vocabulary list. You saw в used a good deal in Диало́г 3. Did you notice what happened to the ending of each word following в?

Masculine	**Feminine**
(институ́т) в институ́те	(шко́ла) в шко́ле
(теа́тр) в теа́тре	(поликли́ника) в поликли́нике
(Но́вгород) в Но́вгороде	(Москва́) в Москве́

Masculine words generally add the ending -е and feminine words replace the ending -а with -е.

2 HOW TO SAY WHICH THING (DEMONSTRATIVE PRONOUNS): *THIS* OR *THAT*

Did you notice in Диало́г 1 that Fiona was told to fill in this form Запо́лните э́тот бланк? Э́тот is the word for *this* or *that* which is used to point out masculine words. So, Да́йте, пожа́луйста, э́тот чемода́н would mean *Please give me that suitcase*. For a feminine noun, use э́та instead. *This girl is my daughter* would be Э́та де́вушка – моя́ дочь. For neuter words you need to use э́то, as in Покажи́те, пожа́луйста, э́то ра́дио *Please show me that radio*. To refer to plural nouns use э́ти, as in

Э́ти биле́ты – мои́. *These tickets are mine.*

3 HOW TO TALK ABOUT ГРАЖДА́НСТВО (GRAZHDÁNSTVA): *NATIONALITY*

In Диало́г 3 you met people of different nationalities. There are different words in Russian to refer to men and women of a particular nationality.

05.06 **Listen as you look at the words then listen again and repeat.**

	Country	Man	Woman	Language
	(страна́)	(мужчи́на)	(же́нщина)	(язы́к)
Russia	Росси́я	ру́сский	ру́сская	по-ру́сски
	Rasséeya	róosky	róoskaya	pa-róosky
England	Англия	англича́нин	англича́нка	по-англи́йски
	Angleeya	angleechánin	angleechánka	pa-angléesky
America	Аме́рика	америка́нец	америка́нка	по-англи́йски
	Amyéreeka	amereekányets	amereekánka	pa-angléesky
Japan	Япо́ния	япо́нец	япо́нка	по-япо́нски
	Yapóniya	yapónyets	yapónka	pa-yapónsky
Spain	Испа́ния	испа́нец	испа́нка	по-испа́нски
	Eespániya	eespányets	eespánka	pa-eespánsky
France	Фра́нция	францу́з	францу́женка	по-францу́зски
	Frántsiya	frantsóos	frantsóozhenka	pa-frantsóozsky
Germany	Герма́ния	не́мец	не́мка	по-неме́цки
	Germániya	nyémyets	nyémka	pa-nemyétsky

Try it!

Now make up sentences to practice:

Вы ру́сский? Вы, коне́чно, говори́те по-ру́сски!

4 HOW TO SAY THE RUSSIAN ALPHABET

While in Russia, you may need to know the names of Russian letters to spell something, for example your name or the name of your home town, so here they are in their correct order.

05.07 Alphabet guide

Listen to the letters as you read them and repeat them out loud. Read top to bottom. There are 3 columns.

The Russian alphabet								
А а	а	*а*	К к	ка	(*ka*)	Х х	ха	(*kha*)
Б б	бэ	(*beh* as in *bed*)	Л л	эль	(*el'*)	Ц ц	цэ	(*tse*)
В в	вэ	(*veh*)	М м	эм	(*em*)	Ч ч	че	(*che*)
Г г	гэ	(*geh*)	Н н	эн	(*en*)	Ш ш	ша	(*sha*)
Д д	дэ	(*deh*)	О́ о	о	(*o*)	Щ щ	ща	(*shsha*)
Е е	е	(*yeh*)	П п	пэ	(*peh*)	ъ	твёрдый знак	(*tvyórdy znak*, hard sign)
Ё ё	ё	(*yoh*)	Р р	эр	(*air*)	ы	ы	(*iy*)
Ж ж	жэ	(*zheh*)	С с	эс	(*es*)	ь	мя́гкий знак	(*myákhky znak*, soft sign)
З з	зэ	(*zeh*)	Т т	тэ	(*teh*)	Э́ э	э	(*eh*)
И и	и	(*ee*)	У у	у	(*oo*)	Ю ю	ю	(*yoo*)
Й й	и кра́ткое	(*ee krátkoye*, short и)	Ф ф	эф	(*ef*)	Я я	я	(*ya*)

Your turn!

Listen to the alphabet again and try to imitate the pronunciation of the speaker. Then glance through the book, picking words at random and spelling them out loud.

5 05.08 NUMBERS 100–1,000

Listen and read the numbers then listen again and repeat.

Numerals 100–1,000

100	сто	**sto**	600	шестьсо́т	**shes-sót**
200	две́сти	**dvyéstee**	700	семьсо́т	**syemsót**
300	три́ста	**tréesta**	800	восемьсо́т	**vasyemsót**
400	четы́реста	**chitíryesta**	900	девятьсо́т	**dyevitsót**
500	пятьсо́т	**pitsót**	1,000	ты́сяча	**týsyacha**

1,539 ты́сяча пятьсо́т три́дцать де́вять **týsyacha pitsót tréetsat' dyévyat'**

Practice

1 05.09 **You're staying in a Russian city when a friend calls asking for phone numbers of hotels there. Read the names and numbers out loud for your friend then listen to the recording to check your answers.**

a Асто́рия 311–42–06

b Евро́па 312–00–72

c Каре́лия 226–35–15

d Оли́мпия 119–68–00

e Санкт-Петербу́рг 542–94–11

f Коммодо́р 119–66–66

2 Tony has to fill in a анке́та (*registration form*) **at the hotel reception desk. Match the information required with his personal details. He spells out his details for the администра́тор to be clearer. Read the spellings out loud.**

a Фами́лия

b Имя

c А́дрес

d Гражда́нство

e Профе́ссия

f Но́мер па́спорта

1 Англича́нин

2 Ка́ртер

3 Тре́нер

4 Антони

5 Р 243569 О

6 Англия, Сто́кпорт, Э́дуард Стрит, дом 35.

3 See if you can guess what nationality these people are.

a шотла́ндец/шотла́ндка

b португа́лец/португа́лка

c ирла́ндец/ирла́ндка

d норве́жец/норве́жка

4 Look at the following jumbled up table of information about four people. You are told their и́мя (*name*), **гражда́нство** (*nationality*), **профе́ссия** (*job*) **and где рабо́тает** (*where he/she works*). **Sort the information so that a French person with a French name is working in a French city. Then make up a sentence about each person. The first one has been done for you:**

Example: а Мари́ – францу́женка. Она́ врач. Она́ рабо́тает в больни́це в Пари́же.

Имя	Гражда́нство	Профе́ссия	Где рабо́тает
a Мари́	**i** ру́сский	**1** учи́тель	**A** в теа́тре в Арха́нгельске
b Ханс	**ii** францу́женка	**2** актёр	**B** в шко́ле в Берли́не
c Бори́с	**iii** англича́нка	**3** продавщи́ца	**C** в больни́це в Пари́же
d Дже́нни	**iv** не́мец	**4** врач	**D** в магази́не в Бирминге́ме

5 Match the questions and answers so that they make sense.

a	Где вы рабо́таете?	**1**	Моя́ фами́лия Бра́дли.
b	Кто вы по профе́ссии?	**2**	Иди́те пря́мо и буфе́т нале́во.
c	Как попа́сть в буфе́т?	**3**	Я рабо́таю в шко́ле.
d	Вы говори́те по-англи́йски?	**4**	Нет, магази́н закры́т.
e	Как ва́ша фами́лия?	**5**	Я врач.
f	Магази́н откры́т?	**6**	Меня́ зову́т Серге́й.
g	Как вас зову́т?	**7**	Нет, я говорю́ по-францу́зски.

6 Remembering that after в and на (meaning *in* or *at*) you have to change the ending of the following word, choose the correct form in these sentences.

a Я рабо́таю в больни́ца/больни́це в Арха́нгельске/Арха́нгельск.

b – Где футболи́сты? – Футболи́сты на стадио́н/стадио́не.

c В гости́нице/гости́ница есть буфе́т?

d – Молодо́й челове́к, где здесь бар? – Бар внизу́, в рестора́н/рестора́не.

7 Choose the correct demonstrative form in these sentences.

a (Э́тот/Э́та/Э́то/Э́ти) кни́га о́чень интере́сная.

b Покажи́те, пожа́луйста, (э́тот/э́та/э́то/э́ти) па́спорт.

c (Э́тот/Э́та/Э́то/Э́ти) журналы не мои́. они́ ва́ши.

d Да́йте, пожа́луйста, (э́тот/э́та/э́то/э́ти) ра́дио.

Go further

NUMBERS AND NAMES

1 Read out the international dialling codes. Then match the countries in Russian with their English equivalents.

a	Австра́лия **61**	1	Germany
b	Бангладе́ш **880**	2	Canada
c	Болга́рия **359**	3	Fiji
d	Гайа́на **592**	5	Israel
e	Герма́ния **49**	6	Ethiopia
f	Изра́иль **972**	7	Australia
g	Кана́да **1**	8	Bulgaria
h	Сингапу́р **65**	9	Guyana
i	Фи́джи **679**	10	Singapore
j	Эфио́пия **251**	11	Bangladesh

2 Unscramble this mixed-up dialogue between a hotel administrator and a tourist called Richard Rigby.

	Администра́тор		**Ри́чард Ри́гби**
a	_______ Вы америка́нец?	e	_______ У вас есть ко́мната?
b	_______ Запо́лните э́тот бланк, пожа́луйста.	f	_______ Здра́вствуйте.
c	_______ Слу́шаю вас	g	_______ Нет, я англича́нин.
d	_______ Да. Как вас зову́т?	h	_______ Меня́ зову́т Ри́чард Ри́гби.

Your turn!

Now give your name, phone number and country to the administrator and spell out your name. Do it phonetically, based on the way your name sounds, not how it is spelled in English.

Test yourself

1 What do these words and phrases mean?

- **a** Мо́жно?
- **b** Где вы рабо́таете?
- **c** Я живу́ в Москве́.
- **d** Как э́то пи́шется?
- **e** Я ру́сский.

2 How would you say these words and phrases in Russian? Say your answers out loud then check them in the back of the book.

- **a** One moment.
- **b** I work in a shop.
- **c** Do you speak English?
- **d** Is the shop open?
- **e** 596

3 What nationality and gender are these people?

- **a** америка́нец
- **b** не́мец
- **c** францу́женка
- **d** ру́сский
- **e** япо́нка
- **f** англича́нка

SELF CHECK

	I CAN...
○	... book into a hotel.
○	... say the alphabet and fill in a form.
○	... talk about where I'm from.
○	... talk about what I do.
○	... say which one I mean, 'this' or 'that'.
○	... count to a thousand.

6

In this unit, you will learn how to:

» tell the time.
» say the days of the week.
» talk about meals and daily routine.
» make arrangements.

Кото́рый час?

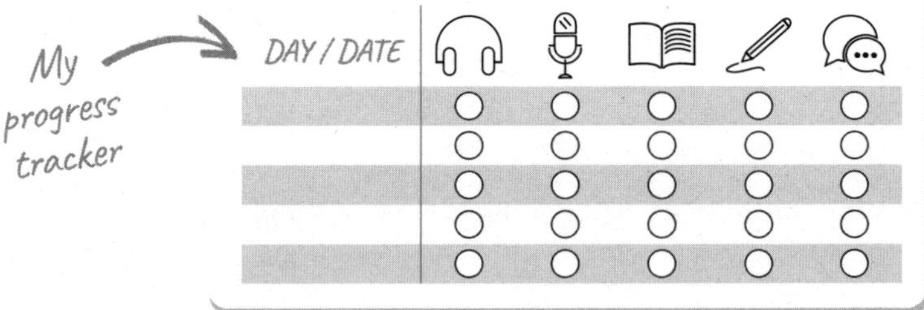

Telling the time

Telling the time in Russia has changed over the years. There are now 11 time zones in Russia. To ask the time, say Кото́рый час? **Katóry chas?** (lit. *Which hour?*) or Ско́лько сейча́с вре́мени? **Skól'ka syeychás vryémyinee?** (lit. *How much now time?*), or to give the time, say, for example, Сейча́с час **Syeychás chas** (*Now it's one o'clock*).

Breakfast, dinner, supper

Like most Europeans, Russians eat meals in the morning, around midday and in the evening: за́втрак **záftrak** (*breakfast*) perhaps with ка́ша **kásha** (*porridge*), meat, cheese or eggs and tea or coffee; and обе́д **abyét** (*dinner*), the main meal, usually at midday or later in the afternoon with заку́ски **zakóosky** (*starters*) if it's a special occasion, a soup and main dish, followed by a dessert and tea or coffee. у́жин **óozhin** (*supper*) is a light evening meal. Хлеб **khlyep** (*bread*) is usually served with all meals.

What is чёрный хлеб chórny khlyep and what is бе́лый хлеб byély khlyep?

Vocabulary builder

06.01 Listen as you look at the words, then listen again and try to imitate the speakers.

NEW EXPRESSIONS

когда́	kagdá	*when*
музе́й открыва́ется	moozyéy atkriváyetsa	*the museum opens*
выходно́й день	vykhadnóydyen'	*day off*
вто́рник	ftórneek	*Tuesday*
музе́й-кварти́ра	moozyéy-kvartéera	*former flat preserved as a museum*
среда́	sryidá	*Wednesday*
зоологи́ческий музе́й	za-alagéechesky moozyéy	*zoological museum*
по́здно	pózdna	*late*
пя́тница	pyátneetsa	*Friday*
конце́рт начина́ется	kantsyért nachináyetsa	*the concert begins*
четве́рг	chitvyérk	*Thursday*
ра́но	rána	*early*
ка́ждый день	kázhdy dyen'	*every day*
у́тром	óotrum	*in the morning*
я встаю́	ya fstayóo	*I get up.*
я за́втракаю	ya záftrakayoo	*I have breakfast.*
я иду́	ya eedóo	*I go* (on foot in one direction)
рабо́та (на)	rabóta	*work*
я обе́даю	ya abyédayoo	*I have dinner.*
ве́чером	vyéchirom	*in the evening*
я у́жинаю	ya óozhinayoo	*I have supper.*
я смотрю́	ya smatryóo	*I watch.*
я ложу́сь спать	ya lazhóos' spat'	*I go to bed.*

Диало́ги *Dialogues*

Listen to the conversations and answer the questions. Then listen again and repeat.

ДИАЛО́Г 1 *DIALOGUE 1*

06.02 *Steven is visiting his friend Marat in St Petersburg for a week. They're trying to plan their time. There are several museums which Steven wants to visit, but first he must find out which выходно́й день* **vykhadnóy dyen'** *(day off) each museum has. Marat looks through the visitors' guide for details.*

1 How many museums does Steven ask about?

Сти́вен	Когда́ открыва́ется ру́сский музе́й?
Марат	Ру́сский музе́й открыва́ется в 10 часо́в. Выходно́й день – вто́рник.
Сти́вен	И музе́й-кварти́ра Пу́шкина?
Марат	Одну́ мину́точку. Да, музе́й-кварти́ра Пу́шкина открыва́ется в 10 часо́в. Выходно́й день – среда́.
Сти́вен	И когда́ открыва́ется зоологи́ческий музе́й?
Марат	Зоологи́ческий музе́й открыва́ется по́здно, в 11 часо́в. Выходно́й день – пя́тница.

2 List the museums that Steven is interested in.

____

____

3 When are the museums closed? Answer (T) for true or (F) for false.

a They are all closed in the mornings.
b One is closed on Fridays.
c One is closed on Mondays and Thursdays.

> Russians are polite but they have their own conventions. For example, Russians say *please* пожа́луйста and *thank you* спаси́бо a lot less than some English-speaking cultures. If you offer a visiting Russian a cup of tea, for instance, they may just say *no* нет.

ДИАЛО́Г 2 *DIALOGUE 2*

06.03 *When they've planned their days, the two friends think about what to do in the evenings.*

1 What do they want to do in the evenings?

Сти́вен	Когда́ начина́ется конце́рт?
Марат	Конце́рт в четве́рг. Он начина́ется ра́но, в 6 часо́в.
Сти́вен	И когда́ начина́ется фильм?
Марат	Ка́ждый день фильм начина́ется в 4 часа́ и в 7 часо́в.

2 Which two pieces of information do they find out about each activity?

ДИАЛО́Г 3 *DIALOGUE 3*

06.04 *Steven wants to fit in with Marat's life, so Marat tells him about his daily routine.*

1 Where does Marat work?

Марат	У́тром я встаю́ в 8 часо́в и за́втракаю в 9 часо́в. Пото́м я иду́ на рабо́ту в библиоте́ку. Библиоте́ка открыва́ется в 10 часо́в. Я там обе́даю, и ве́чером я у́жинаю до́ма в 7 часо́в. Пото́м я смотрю́ телеви́зор и по́здно ложу́сь спать.

2 Answer the questions.

a What time does Marat get up?

b When does he have breakfast?

c Where does he have the main meal of the day?

3 What does he like to do in the evening? Find the phrase in the conversation that expresses Marat's evening leisure activity.

06.05 Learn these phrases about making arrangements before going to the conversation! Listen as you read then listen again and repeat.

Где мы встре́тимся?	**Gdye my fstryétimsa?**	*Where shall we meet?*
за́л Филармо́нии	**zal Feelarmónee**	*Philharmonic hall*
Встре́тимся	**Fstryétimsa**	*Let's meet*

ДИАЛО́Г 4 *DIALOGUE 4*

06.06 *Before Marat leaves for work, Steven asks where they should meet before going to the concert.*

1 Where does Marat suggest they should meet?

Сти́вен	Где мы встре́тимся?
Марат	Конце́рт начина́ется в 6 часо́в в за́ле Филармо́нии. Встре́тимся в 5 часо́в в библиоте́ке. Мо́жно, Сти́вен?
Сти́вен	Мо́жно.

2 Read the conversation out loud line by line.

3 Cover up the conversation and complete the missing words.

Конце́рт начина́ется в 6 часо́в в за́ле Филармо́нии.
________ в 5 ________ ________ библиоте́ке. ________,Сти́вен?

4 You and a friend are going to the зоологи́ческий музе́й on Friday. Send an email and ask where you should meet.

Новое сообщение

От:

Кому:

Тема:

Language discovery

1 TELLING THE TIME

To ask the time, say Кото́рый час? **Katóry chas?** (lit. *Which hour?*) or Ско́лько сейча́с вре́мени? **Skól'ka syeychás vryémyinee?** (lit. *How much now time?*) Look at the exact times given below.

06.07 Listen and repeat.

1.00	сейча́с час	**syeychás chas**
2.00	сейча́с два часа́	**syeychás dva chasá**
3.00	три часа́	**tree chasá**
4.00	четы́ре часа́	**chitýrye chasá**
5.00	пять часо́в	**pyat' chasóf**
6.00	шесть часо́в	**shest' chasóf**
7.00	семь часо́в	**syem' chasóf**
8.00	во́семь часо́в	**vósyem' chasóf**
9.00	де́вять часо́в	**dyévyat' chasóf**
10.00	де́сять часо́в	**dyésyat' chasóf**
11.00	оди́ннадцать часо́в	**adéenatsat' chasóf**
12.00	двена́дцать часо́в	**dvyenátsat' chasóf**

по́лдень **póldyen'** *midday* по́лночь **pólnoch'** *midnight*

Час means *hour*. A *watch* or *clock* is часы́ (lit. *hours*). Did you notice that час has different endings depending on which number it follows? After one: час; after two, three and four: часа́; and after 5–20: часо́в. To complete the 24-hour clock, after 21: час; and after 22, 23 and 24: часа́.

В кото́ром часу́? *At what time?* В пять часо́в. *At five o'clock.*

Telling the time on the hour is easy: сейча́с час **syeychás chas** (*now it's one o'clock*), or сейча́с два часа́ **syeychás dva chasá** (*now it's two o'clock*).

Telling the time not on the hour can be done in a number of ways, but the easiest is to do it digitally, for example 10.20 is де́сять часо́в два́дцать мину́т and 4.45 is четы́ре часа́ со́рок пять мину́т.

2 DAYS OF THE WEEK

06.08 Listen and repeat.

понеде́льник	**panidyél'neek**	*Monday*
вто́рник	**ftórneek**	*Tuesday*
среда́	**sryidá**	*Wednesday*
четве́рг	**chitvyérk**	*Thursday*
пя́тница	**pyátneetsa**	*Friday*
суббо́та	**soobóta**	*Saturday*
воскресе́нье	**vaskrisyén'ye**	*Sunday*

Notice that the days of the week and months are in lower-case letters in Russian. To ask what day it is, say Како́й сего́дня день? **Kakóy sivódnya dyen'?** Also, the word сего́дня (*today*) is not pronounced as it is spelled; г is pronounced as a в. To say what day it is, say сего́дня суббо́та **sivódnya soobóta** (*today is Saturday*). If you want to say *on* a day of the week, use в. If the day of the week ends in -a, change -a to -y, for example, в суббо́ту.

в понеде́льник	**fpanidyél'neek**	*on Monday*
во вто́рник	**vo vtórneek**	*on Tuesday*
в сре́ду	**fsryédoo**	*on Wednesday*
в четве́рг	**fchitvyérk**	*on Thursday*
в пя́тницу	**fpyátneetsoo**	*on Friday*
в суббо́ту	**fsoobótoo**	*on Saturday*
в воскресе́нье	**v-vaskrisyén'ye**	*on Sunday*

To say *on Wednesday* the stress changes: from среда́ to в сре́ду.

3 ORDINAL NUMBERS: FIRST, SECOND, THIRD ...

To form Russian ordinal numbers, add an adjective ending to the numerals you already know, once you get past the first few. Following are the ordinal numerals for 1–10 in their masculine forms, for use with masculine nouns (деся́тый эта́ж **disyáty etásh** (*tenth floor*)).

Ordinal numbers 1st–10th

1st	пе́рвый	**pyérvy**	*6th*	шесто́й	**shestóy**
2nd	второ́й	**ftaróy**	*7th*	седьмо́й	**syidmóy**
3rd	тре́тий	**tryéty**	*8th*	восьмо́й	**vas'móy**
4th	четвёртый	**chitvyórty**	*9th*	девя́тый	**divyáty**
5th	пя́тый	**pyáty**	*10th*	деся́тый	**disyáty**

Practice

1 06.09 Listen and give the times in numbers that places open and events begin.

- **a** Бассе́йн открыва́ется в ...
- **b** О́пера начина́ется в ...
- **c** Буфе́т открыва́ется в ...
- **d** Марафо́н начина́ется в ...
- **e** Галере́я открыва́ется в ..
- **f** Конце́рт начина́ется в ...
- **g** Зоопа́рк открыва́ется в ...
- **h** Моя́ рабо́та начина́ется в ..
- **i** Фильм начина́ется в ...

2 Give these times in Russian. Say them out loud.

a

b

c

d

e

f

g

h

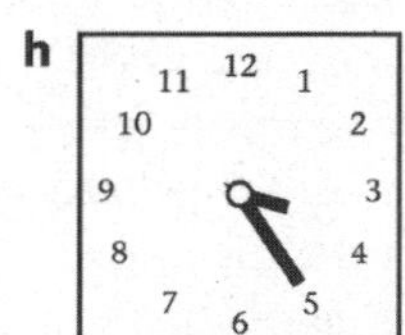

i

3 **Look at the clocks and complete the captions. Use the verbs in the box if needed.**

встаю́ иду́ обе́даю за́втракаю смотрю́

- **a** В ________ часо́в я ________.
- **b** В ________ часо́в я ________.
- **c** В ________ часо́в я ________ на рабо́ту.
- **d** В час я ________ на рабо́те.
- **e** В ________ часо́в я у́жинаю до́ма.
- **f** В ________ часо́в я ________ телеви́зор.
- **g** В ________ часо́в я ложу́сь спать.

4 **Read the details of these St Petersburg museums. Tell your Russian friend when they open, what day they close and their phone numbers.**

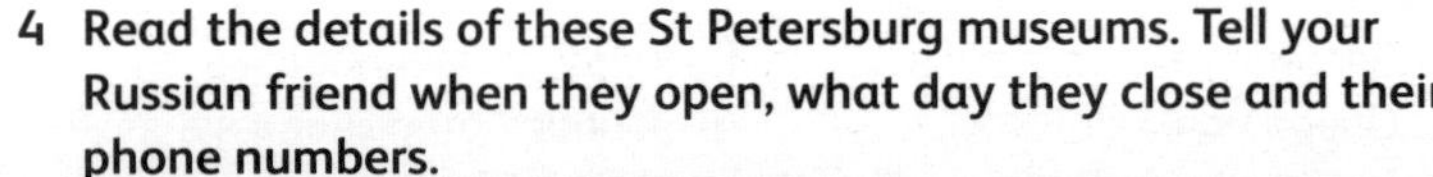

	Time of opening	Day off	Phone number
a Museum of Anthropology and Ethnography Музе́й антрополо́гии и этногра́фии	11.00	Sat	218-14-12
b Museum of Musical Instruments Музе́й музыка́льных инструме́нтов	12.00	Tues	314-53-55
c Museum Apartment of A. A. Blok Музе́й-кварти́ра А. А. Бло́ка	11.00	Wed	113-86-33
d Museum of the Arctic and Antarctic Музе́й а́рктики и анта́рктики	10.00	Mon	311-25-49

5 **Anna is very busy. She listed who and what for each day in her diary and wrote a note of times and places to meet. Put the correct day of the week for each note.**

Пн.	Вт.	Ср	Чт.	Пт.	Сб.	Вс.
Са́ша	Та́ня	Гульнара	Руслан	Ма́ша	Ди́ма	Кири́лл
фильм	обе́д	О́пера	футбо́л	экску́рсия	конце́рт	джаз

- **a** ________ Встре́тимся на стадио́не в 3 часа́.
- **b** ________ Встре́тимся в кинотеа́тре в 7 часо́в.
- **c** ________ Встре́тимся до́ма в 6 часо́в.
- **d** ________ Встре́тимся в теа́тре о́перы и бале́та в 7 часо́в.
- **e** ________ Встре́тимся в за́ле Филармо́нии в 6 часо́в.
- **f** ________ Встре́тимся в це́нтре джа́зовой му́зыки в 2 часа́.
- **g** ________ Встре́тимся в авто́бусе в час.

6 **Match each item with the department store floor where it is sold.**

a contact lenses
b perfume
c a saxophone
d a matryoshka doll
e a safe
f a book
g a printer
h linoleum
i lipstick

________ Шестóй этáж: книги.

________ Пя́тый этáж: Сéйфы. Линóлеум. Сувени́ры.

________ Четвёртый этáж: нóутбуки, при́нтеры, телеви́зоры, мобильные телефоны

________ Трéтий этáж: Музыкáльные инструмéнты. Фóто.

________ Второ́й этáж: Парфюмéрия. Космéтика.

________ Пéрвый этáж: Гомеопати́ческая аптéка. Óптика – контáктные ли́нзы.

7 **Read the sentences and choose the correct endings, depending on whether в and на mean to or in.**

a Я рабóтаю в теáтр/теáтре в Нóвгород/Нóвгороде.
b Я иду́ в библиотéку/библиотéке.
c Вы рабóтаете в университéт/университéте или в шкóлу/шкóле?
d – Кудá вы идёте? – Я иду́ в институ́т/институ́те.
e Извини́те, пожáлуйста. Как попáсть в поликли́нику/поликли́нике?

8 **06.10 Anna is talking about things she does every day of the week. Listen and complete the sentences with the correct day of the week in English, and then say each sentence out loud in Russian.**

a В ________ я рабóтаю в институ́те.
b В ________ я обéдаю в ресторáне.
c В ________ вéчером я смотрю́ телеви́зор.
d В ________ я встаю́ рáно и слу́шаю рáдио.
e В ________ у́тром я иду́ в библиотéку. Потóм в 2 часá я иду́ в институ́т.
f В ________ я ложу́сь спать óчень пóздно.
g В ________ я встаю́ и зáвтракаю пóздно.

Test yourself

1 Choose the word or phrase that does NOT belong in each group.

a (*days of the week*) вто́рник, среда́, музе́й, четве́рг

b (*times of day*) я встаю́, у́тром, ве́чером, ра́но

c (*routines*) я встаю́, я обе́даю, я смотрю́, конце́рт

d (*clock times*) семь часо́в, три часа́, де́вять часо́в, ка́ша

e (*meals*) за́втрак, у́жин, спаси́бо, обе́д

f (*getting together*) встре́тимся , хлеб, когда́, суббо́та

2 How would you say the following in Russian? Say your answers out loud and check the answers in the back of the book.

a Say the days of the week in their correct order and then in reverse order.

b Say what time it is now. (Ask yourself this question throughout the day!)

c How would you ask *When does the bank open?*

d Ask *When does the film start?*

e Tell a friend *Let's meet at 7 o'clock at the restaurant*.

f The breakfast menu says ка́ша, мю́сли, хлеб, ко́фе. What are you being offered?

g Say that you get up at seven o'clock.

h Say that you watch television in the evening.

i Say that you work in Moscow.

j Say that you are going to the theater.

SELF CHECK

	I CAN...
◯	... tell the time.
◯	... say the days of the week.
◯	... talk about meals and daily routine.
◯	... make arrangements.

R2 Review 2

1 Translate the sentences to complete the conversation in Russian.

You	*Do you have green tea?*
Server	Извини́те, нет.
You	*What do you have?*
Server	Ко́фе, пе́пси-ко́ла, минера́льная вода́ и фрукто́вый сок.
You	*Give me fruit juice, please.*
Server	Фрукто́вый сок. Сейча́с.

Points: _______ /3

2 Say these phone numbers out loud.

a 172 – 45 – 98
b 313 – 64 – 59
c 536 – 14 – 72
d 853 – 81 – 12

Points: _______ / 4

3 What are these question words in Russian?

a How?
b What?
c Who?
d Where?
e When?
f Where to?

Points: _______ /6

4 Choose the correct forms of the words *my* and *your* in the conversations below.

a Это (ваш/ва́ша/ва́ше/ва́ши) ключ?
Нет, э́то не (мой/моя́/моё/мои́) ключ.

b Это (мой/моя́/моё/мои́) газе́та.
Нет, э́то не (ваш/ва́ша/ва́ше/ва́ши) газе́та. Э́то (мой/моя́/моё/мои́) газе́та.

c Э́то (ваш/ва́ша/ва́ше/ва́ши) ра́дио?
Да, э́то (мой/моя́/моё/мои́) ра́дио.

d Это (ваш/ва́ша/ва́ше/ва́ши) конфе́ты?
Нет, э́то не (мой/моя́/моё/мои́) конфе́ты.

Points: _______ /9

5 Imagine you are at a hotel reception. Answer the administrator's questions in Russian.

a Как ва́ша фами́лия?
b Как э́то пи́шется?
c Како́й у вас а́дрес?
d Кто вы по профе́ссии?
e Како́е у вас гражда́нство?

Points: _______ /5

6 Where do these people want to go and what directions are they given? In English, put your answers in the blanks.

a

A	Как попа́сть в университе́т?
B	Иди́те пря́мо, пото́м напра́во и университе́т недалеко́.

____

b

A	Как попа́сть на вокза́л?
B	Иди́те нале́во.
A	Это далеко́?
B	Мину́т де́сять.

____

c

A	Как попа́сть в библиоте́ку?
B	Вот она́.

____

Points: _______ /6

7 Read the notices. Say what is happening and when.

a Концéрт начинáется в вóсемь часóв.

b Музéй открывáется в дéсять часóв.

c Зáвтрак начинáется в шесть часóв трúдцать минут.

d В понедéльник теáтр закры́т.

Points: _______ /4

8 Where are these people going to meet and at what time? Choose the correct answer.

a Встрéтимся на стадиóне в 2 часá.
- **1** stadium 2.00
- **2** cinema Saturday the 2nd

b Встрéтимся в гостúнице в 8 часóв.
- **1** café 8 am
- **2** hotel 8.00

c Встрéтимся в библиотéке в 5 часóв.
- **1** restaurant 5 pm.
- **2** library 5.00

d Встрéтимся в кафé в час.
- **1** café 1.00
- **2** cinema noon

e Встрéтимся на вокзáле в 4 часá.
- **1** train station 4.00
- **2** train station (on) the 4th

f Встрéтимся в кинотеáтре в 7 часóв.
- **1** cinema 7.00
- **2** library 7 pm.

Points: _______ /6

9 Put the days of the week in the correct order, starting with Monday.

субббота

вто́рник

четве́рг

воскресе́нье

пя́тница

понеде́льник

среда́

Points: ______ /7

Total points: ______ /50

7

In this unit, you will learn how to:

» talk about leisure activities and holidays.
» say the date.
» talk about likes and dislikes.
» use verbs in different forms.
» say numerals over 1,000.

Вы лю́бите спорт?

My progress tracker

DAY / DATE	Listening	Speaking	Reading	Writing	Conversation
	○	○	○	○	○
	○	○	○	○	○
	○	○	○	○	○
	○	○	○	○	○
	○	○	○	○	○

Public holidays

Here are a few of the пра́здники **prázdneeky** (*public holidays*) celebrated in Russia:

Но́вый год **Nóvy got**, 1 января́ (*New Year, 1 January*)
Рождество́ **Razhdyestvó**, 7 января́ (*Orthodox Christmas, 7 January*)
Же́нский день **Zhénsky dyen'**, 8 ма́рта (*Women's Day, 8 March*)
День Побе́ды **Dyen' pabyédy**, 9 ма́я (*Victory Day, 9 May, end of WWII*

The greeting с пра́здником **s prázdneekum** (lit. *with the holiday: I congratulate you with the holiday*) applies to any occasion. To offer good wishes for the new year, say с но́вым го́дом **s nóvym gódum** (*Happy New Year*). On New Year's Eve, Дед Моро́з **Dyet Marós** (*Grandfather Frost*) with his helper Снегу́рочка the **Snyigóoruchka** (*Snowmaiden*) gives out presents by the ёлка **yólka** (*tree*). Russians celebrate Orthodox Christmas on the 7th of January according to the Julian calendar, 13 days later than the Gregorian calendar used by Catholic and Protestant churches.

What is this public holiday and when is it celebrated: День Росси́и, двена́дцатого ию́ня.

Vocabulary builder

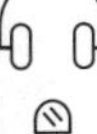

07.01 Listen as you look at the words, then listen again and try to imitate the speakers.

MONTHS OF THE YEAR

The months of the year are all masculine.

янва́рь	yinvár'	*January*	**ию́ль**	eeyóol'	*July*
февра́ль	fyevrál'	*February*	**а́вгуст**	avgoost	*August*
март	mart	*March*	**сентя́брь**	syentyábr'	*September*
апре́ль	apryél'	*April*	**октя́брь**	aktyábr'	*October*
май	maee	*May*	**ноя́брь**	nayábr'	*November*
ию́нь	eeyóon'	*June*	**дека́брь**	dyekábr'	*December*

NEW EXPRESSIONS

хо́бби	khóbbee	*hobby*
вы чита́ете	vy cheetáyetye	*you read*
я чита́ю	ya cheetáyoo	*I read.*
газе́та	gazyéta	*newspaper*
то́же	tózhe	*also*
рома́н	ramán	*novel*
интере́сно	intiryésna	*that's interesting*
я игра́ю в бадминто́н	ya eegráyoo v badmeentón	*I play badminton.*
гуля́ть	goolyát'	*to go for a walk*
му́зыка	móozyka	*music*
я игра́ю на саксофо́не	ya eegráyoo na saksafónye	*I play the saxophone.*
ходи́ть на конце́рты	khadéet' na kantsyérty	*to go to concerts*
путеше́ствовать	pootyishéstvuvat'	*to travel*
пя́тое октября́	pyátoye aktyabryá	*5th of October*
Вы хоти́те пойти́?	Vy khatéetye paeetée?	*Do you want to go?*

Try saying *Happy Birthday* in Russian – с днём рожде́ния **s dnyom razhdyéniya** (lit. *with the day of birth*).

Диало́ги *Dialogues*

Listen to the conversations and answer the questions. Then listen again and repeat.

ДИАЛО́Г 1 *DIALOGUE 1*

Part 1

07.02A *George is introduced to Lyudmila, and they talk about their leisure interests.*

1 What interests does George have?

Людми́ла	Каки́е у вас хо́бби?
Джордж	Я о́чень люблю́ чита́ть.
Людми́ла	Чита́ть? Каки́е кни́ги вы чита́ете?
Джордж	Ка́ждый день я чита́ю газе́ты, и я то́же люблю́ чита́ть рома́ны.
Людми́ла	Интере́сно. Вы лю́бите ру́сские рома́ны?
Джордж	Да, о́чень люблю́. А вы, у вас есть хо́бби?
Людми́ла	Да, но я совсе́м не люблю́ чита́ть! Я люблю́ спорт. Я игра́ю в бадминто́н и в те́ннис, и я люблю́ гуля́ть.

2 Find the words in the conversation that mean *I read newspapers*.

3 Does Lyudmila share George's interests?

4 What are Lyudmila's favorite activities?

____

____

____

____

5 Tell George that you like to read magazines and play football. (Hint: *a magazine* is журна́л zhoornál – be careful to say magazines in the plural form and not just magazine; *football* is футбо́л footból.)

Part 2

07.02B *They continue their conversation ...*

6 What musical interest do George and Lyudmila find that they share?

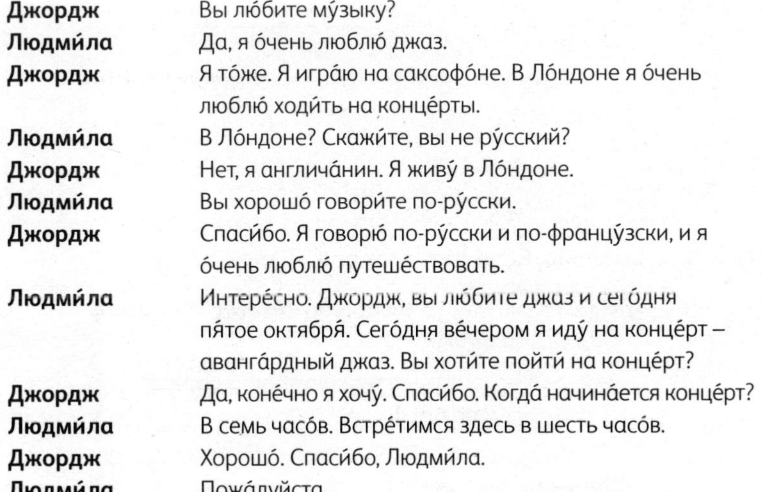

Джордж	Вы лю́бите му́зыку?
Людми́ла	Да, я о́чень люблю́ джаз.
Джордж	Я то́же. Я игра́ю на саксофо́не. В Ло́ндоне я о́чень люблю́ ходи́ть на конце́рты.
Людми́ла	В Ло́ндоне? Скажи́те, вы не ру́сский?
Джордж	Нет, я англича́нин. Я живу́ в Ло́ндоне.
Людми́ла	Вы хорошо́ говори́те по-ру́сски.
Джордж	Спаси́бо. Я говорю́ по-ру́сски и по-францу́зски, и я о́чень люблю́ путеше́ствовать.
Людми́ла	Интере́сно. Джордж, вы лю́бите джаз и сего́дня пя́тое октября́. Сего́дня ве́чером я иду́ на конце́рт – аванга́рдный джаз. Вы хоти́те пойти́ на конце́рт?
Джордж	Да, коне́чно я хочу́. Спаси́бо. Когда́ начина́ется конце́рт?
Людми́ла	В семь часо́в. Встре́тимся здесь в шесть часо́в.
Джордж	Хорошо́. Спаси́бо, Людми́ла.
Людми́ла	Пожа́луйста.

7 Find this phrase in the conversation: Я говорю́ по-францу́зски (Ya gavaryóo pa-frantsóozsky). Study the context. What does it mean?

8 Answer the questions.

a What is Lyudmila surprised to find out about George?

b Where does George live?

c Where does Lyudmila invite George to this evening?

d Where and when do they agree to meet?

9 Lyudmila needs to change plans. What is she saying to George?

✉ Новое сообщение

От:

Кому:

Встре́тимся в ба́ре в гости́нице в семь часо́в. Fstryétimsa v bárye v gastéeneetse v syem' chasóf.

10 Talk to Lyudmila. Read the notes and do the activities.

→ я люблю́ чита́ть **ya lyooblyóo cheetát'** (*I love reading*)

→ я не люблю́ чита́ть **ya nye lyooblyóo cheetát'** (*I don't like reading*)

To emphasize your feelings, add other words to the sentence:

→ я о́чень люблю́ чита́ть **ya óchen' lyooblyóo cheetát'** (*I really love reading*)

→ я совсе́м не люблю́ чита́ть **ya savsyém nye lyooblyóo cheetát'** (*I really don't like reading*)

a Tell her what you like and don't like in English.

Я о́чень люблю́ игра́ть в гольф. **Ya Ochen' lyooblyóo eegrát' v gol'f.**
Я совсе́м не люблю́ ко́фе. **Ya savsyém nye lyooblyóo kófye.**

b Tell her in Russian that you really like doing these things:

Language discovery

Look at the names of these months for forming dates: января́, февраля́, ма́рта, апре́ля. Go back to the list in the Vocabulary builder and compare. What ending is used for months to form dates?

1 КАКО́Е СЕГО́ДНЯ ЧИСЛО́? *WHAT'S THE DATE TODAY?*

Ordinal numbers 1st–31st

Dates are given in ordinal numbers (Unit 6), whose neuter ending -ое agrees with the neuter число́, followed by the month with the ending -а or -я which gives the meaning *of*. Study the ordinal numbers 1st–31st with neuter endings.

07.03 Listen as you look at the numbers then listen again and repeat.

1st	пе́рвое	**pyérvoye**
2nd	второ́е	**ftaróye**
3rd	тре́тье	**tryét'ye**
4th	четвёртое	**chitvyórtoye**
5th	пя́тое	**pyátoye**
6th	шесто́е	**shestóye**
7th	седьмо́е	**syedmóye**
8th	восьмо́е	**vas'móye**
9th	девя́тое	**dyevyátoye**
10th	деся́тое	**dyesyátoye**
11th	оди́ннадцатое	**adéenatsatoye**
12th	двена́дцатое	**dvyenátsatoye**
13th	трина́дцатое	**treenátsatoye**
14th	четы́рнадцатое	**chiti̇́rnatsatoye**
15th	пятна́дцатое	**pitnátsatoye**

Here is the second set.

16th	шестнáдцатое	**shestnátsatoye**
17th	семнáдцатое	**syemnátsatoye**
18th	восемнáдцатое	**vasyemnátsatoye**
19th	девятнáдцатое	**dyevitnátsatoye**
20th	двадцáтое	**dvatsátoye**
21st	двáдцать пéрвое	**dvátsat' pyérvoye**
22nd	двáдцать вторóе	**dvátsat' ftaróye**
30th	тридцáтое	**treetsátoye**
31st	трúдцать пéрвое	**tréetsat' pyérvoye**

▶ Months for forming dates

The months have endings -а or -я for forming dates:

января́	февраля́	мáрта	апрéля
мáя	ию́ня	ию́ля	áвгуста
сентября́	октября́	ноября́	декабря́

So, Сегóдня пя́тое áвгуста means *Today is 5th August*.

двенáдцатое января́	*12 Jan.*	вторóе декабря́	*2 Dec.*
седьмóе мáя	*7 May*	шестóе февраля́	*6 Feb.*
тридцáтое сентября́	*30 Sept.*	девятнáдцатое мáрта	*19 Mar.*

▶ To say on a certain date: the ending of the ordinal numeral should change to -ого, pronounced **-ovo**. An exception to this is трéтьего *on the third*.

Двенáдцатого áвгуста *on 12th August*

▶ To say *in* a month: use в and change the ending of the month to -е.

в январé	в февралé	в мáрте	в апрéле	в мáе	в ию́не
в ию́ле	в áвгусте	в сентябрé	в октябрé	в ноябрé	в декабрé

For *in* + season, say: *in spring* веснóй, *in summer* лéтом, *in fall* óсенью, *in winter* зимóй

2 VERB GROUPS

There are two main groups of verbs in Russian, which we will call Group 1 and Group 2. Note: The infinitive is the dictionary form (in English: *to do, to eat*, etc.).

Group 1

Look at the verb *to work*, a Group 1 verb in Russian. Note that in Russian рабóтать has more changes to endings than in English.

to work (infinitive)	
(singular)	(plural)
I work	we work
you work	you work
he/she/it works	they work

рабóтать (infinitive) *to work*	
(singular)	(plural)
я рабóта**ю***	мы рабóта**ем**
ты рабóта**ешь**	вы рабóта**ете***
он/онá/онó рабóта**ет**	они́ рабóта**ют**

*Verb forms presented in previous units.

Formation: Remove the -ть from the infinitive which ends in ать or ять and add the endings in bold type. This applies to other Group 1 verbs you have met such as знать, понимáть, зáвтракать, обéдать, ýжинать, читáть, игрáть, гуля́ть.

Group 2

You have also met some Group 2 verbs, for example говори́ть.

говори́ть (infinitive) *to speak/talk*	
(singular)	(plural)
я говорю́*	мы говори́м
ты говори́шь	вы говори́те*
он/онá/онó говори́т	они́ говоря́т

Formation: Remove the last three letters from the infinitive which ends in ить or еть and add the endings. Люби́ть is a Group 2 verb but is unusual in the first person singular, where it inserts an л before the ending: я люблю́. In future vocabulary lists, we will identify the verbs as group 1 or 2.

Irregular

Some verbs are irregular, i.e. they do not follow the patterns given above.

хотéть (khatyét') *to want*	
я хочý*	мы хотúм
ты хóчешь	вы хотúте*
он/онá/онó хóчет	онú хотя́т

жить (zheet') *to live* **(Group 1)**	
я живý*	мы живём
ты живёшь	вы живёте*
он/онá/онó живёт	онú живýт

3 HOW TO SAY *I LOVE TO, I WANT TO, I PLAY ...*

- *I love doing something*: Я люблю́ + verb infinitive: e.g. Я люблю́ читáть *I love reading*. And *I love something*: Я люблю́ + noun. As a direct object, the nouns need accusative endings. If it is feminine -a will change to -у and -я to -ю: e.g. Я люблю́ мýзыку *I love music*. If it is masculine or neuter it will not change: e.g. Я люблю́ спорт *I love sport*.
- *I want to do something*: Я хочý + verb infinitive: e.g. Я хочý говорúть по-рýсски *I want to speak Russian*. *I play a sport*: Я игрáю в + sport: e.g. Я игрáю в бадминтóн/в футбóл/в гольф *I play badminton/ football/golf*. Or, *I play an instrument*: Я игрáю на + instrument, using the prepositional ending -е: e.g. Я игрáю на гитáре/на балалáйке *I play the guitar/balalaika*.
- *I* (habitually) *go somewhere*: Я хожý в/на + place. Use an accusative ending. If the place is feminine -a will change to -у and -я to -ю: e.g. Я хожý в больнúцу/на вокзáл *I go to the hospital/station*.

4 CARDINAL NUMBERS 1,000–20,000

07.04 Listen as you read the numbers then listen again and repeat.

1,000	ты́сяча	**týsyacha**
2,000	две ты́сячи	**dvye týsyachee**
3,000	три ты́сячи	**tree týsyachee**
4,000	четы́ре ты́сячи	**chitýrye týsyachee**
5,000	пять ты́сяч	**pyat' týsyach**
6,000	шесть ты́сяч	**shest' týsyach**
7,000	семь ты́сяч	**syem' týsyach**
8,000	вóсемь ты́сяч	**vósyem' týsyach**
9,000	дéвять ты́сяч	**dyévyat' týsyach**
10,000	дéсять ты́сяч	**dyésyat' týsyach**
20,000	двáдцать ты́сяч	**dvátsat' týsyach**

Practice

1 Answer the questions about the cultural events program. For the first event, say: Суббо́та пе́рвое октября́. Пье́са. Оте́лло. (Пье́са is a play).

сб. 1 октября́	Пье́са. Оте́лло
вс. 2 октября́	Пье́са. Три сестры́
пн. 3 октября́	Пье́са. Клау́строфобия
вт. 4 октября́	Опера. Бори́с Годуно́в
ср. 5 октября́	Конце́рт. Джаз группа 'Ми́стер Джаз'
чт. 6 октября́	Конце́рт. Бах, Шу́берт и Шу́ман
пт. 7 октября́	Пье́са. Три мушкетёра

a Which evening could you hear classical music?
b When could you hear jazz?
c What is the title of Chekhov's play on Sunday?
d When is the opera?

2 Look at Valódya's favorite seasonal activities. Match the pictures with the statements below. Put the season in the blank.

1

2

3

4

a Весно́й я люблю́ путеше́ствовать. ________
b Ле́том я люблю́ игра́ть в те́ннис и чита́ть на пля́же. ________
c О́сенью я люблю́ гуля́ть в па́рке. ________
d Зимо́й я люблю́ игра́ть в хокке́й и смотре́ть телеви́зор. ________

3 **Now say what you like doing at different times of year.**

4 **07.05 Listen and say which activities these people like and dislike. You may not catch every word, but try to pick out the relevant details.**

a Boris
b Lisa
c Andrei
d Nina

5 **Read these dates out loud and fill in the blank with how you would say the date in Russian.**

a 1 Jan. – Но́вый год. _______
b 7 Jan. – Рождество́. _______
c 8 March – Же́нский день. _______
d 9 May – День Побе́ды. _______
e Сего́дня _______.
f Мой день рожде́ния (*birthday*) _______.

6 **Write these dates in Russian.**

Example: *13th June* трина́дцатого ию́ня.

a	13th June	24th December	31st October
b	6th September	3rd October	14th February

7 **Choose the correct endings for these verbs.**

a Я рабо́таю/рабо́таете в шко́ле.
b Вы говорю́/говори́те по-ру́сски?
c Я не понима́ете/понима́ю.
d Я люблю́/лю́бите чай с лимо́ном.
e Вы живу́/живёте в Ло́ндоне?
f Ка́ждый день я за́втракаю/за́втракаете до́ма.
g О́сенью я гуля́ю/гуля́ете в па́рке.

8 **07.06 Listen and mark what Андре́й says he likes and dislikes.**

	Я о́чень люблю́	Я люблю́	Я не люблю́	Я совсе́м не люблю́
a Work				
b Sport				
c Music				
d Watching TV				
e Travel				
f Cinema				

Test yourself

1 Read this conversation out loud.

Анто́н	Каки́е у вас хо́бби?
А́нна	Я о́чень люблю́ читать книги и путеше́ствовать.
Анто́н	Интере́сно.
А́нна	А вы, у вас есть хо́бби?
Анто́н	Да, но я совсе́м не люблю́ чита́ть! Я люблю́ спорт. Зимо́й я игра́ю в хокке́й и ле́том я люблю́ гуля́ть.
А́нна	Вы лю́бите му́зыку?
Анто́н	Нет, не о́чень. А вы?
А́нна	Я о́чень люблю́ му́зыку и люблю́ ходи́ть на конце́рты.

2 Answer the following questions. Go back to the conversation if needed.

a What four things does Ánna say she likes?

b What two things does Antón not like?

c What three things does Antón say he likes?

3 Say what you like doing at different times of the day: Утром óotrum (*in the morning*), днём dnyom (*in the afternoon*), ве́чером vyéchirom (*in the evening*), но́чью nóch'yoo (*at night*).

SELF CHECK

	I CAN. . .
○	. . . talk about leisure activities and holidays.
○	. . . say the date.
○	. . . talk about likes and dislikes.
○	. . . use verbs in different forms.
○	. . . say numbers over 1,000.

8

In this unit, you will learn how to:

» talk about home and family (yours and theirs!).
» be a guest in a Russian home.
» plan a route on public transport.

Входи́те, пожа́луйста!

My progress tracker

DAY / DATE	🎧	🎙	📖	✏	💬
	○	○	○	○	○
	○	○	○	○	○
	○	○	○	○	○
	○	○	○	○	○
	○	○	○	○	○

Home and family

A Russian семья́ **sim'yá** (*family*) is a close-knit unit. A Ба́бушка **bábooshka** (*grandmother*) may help bring up children and run the home while parents work. Pre-school children may attend a я́сли **yásly** (*nursery*) or де́тский сад **dyétskee sat** (*kindergarten*). Most people in urban areas live in modern apartments. There are four building classifications: economy, comfort, business and elite. Economy class are the cheapest new Russian apartments – they are the high-rise complexes on the edges of cities. At the other end of the spectrum are elite class apartments. These are the most expensive. They are architect-designed and located in gated compounds close to the city center. They boast spas, gyms and underground parking. Communities of exclusive housing котте́джные посёлки **kotedzhnye posyelki** (*villages*) have sprung up on the edges of cities, and include properties described as a дом **dom** (*house*) or ко́ттедж **kótedzh** (*cottage*) set in secure compounds. In adverts for even modest properties in such communities you will see words such as комфо́рт **komfórt** (*comfort*), ками́н **kaméen** (*a fireplace*) and джаку́зи **djakóozy** (*a jacuzzi*).

Where do the majority of people in Russia live? a кварти́ра b ко́ттедж.

Vocabulary builder

08.01 Listen as you look at the words, then listen again and try to imitate the speakers.

NEW EXPRESSIONS

входи́те	vkhadéetye	*come in*
сади́тесь	sadéetyes'	*sit down*
семья́	sim'yá	*family*
Да, есть.	Da, yest'.	*Yes, I have/he has/they have, etc.*
посмотри́те	pasmatréetye	*look* (imperative)
у меня́ (есть)	oo minyá (yest')	*I have*
альбо́м	al'bóm	*album*
жена́	zhiná	*wife*
муж	moosh	*husband*
де́ти	dyétee	*children*
ви́дите	véedeetye	*you see*
их зову́т	eekh zavóot	*they are called*
маши́на	mashéena	*car*
её зову́т	yiyó zavóot	*she is called*
да́ча (на)	dácha	*dacha (country house)*
мать/оте́ц	mat'/atyéts	*mother/father*
на пе́нсии	na pyénsee	*on a pension (retired)*
их	eekh	*them*
его́ зову́т	yivó zavóot	*he is called*
энерги́чный	inyergéechnee	*energetic*
дере́вня	dyiryévnya	*countryside/village*
дя́дя/тётя	dyádya/tyótya	*uncle/aunt*

When finding your way around a Russian city you may need to consult a plan of bus, trolleybus and tram routes. Major roads on the route will be named. You already know у́лица (*street*), проспе́кт (*avenue*), пло́щадь (*square*) and мост (*bridge*), but here are three more useful words: на́бережная **nábyiryezhnaya** (*embankment*), шоссе́ **shosséy** (*main road*) and река́ **ryiká** (*river*).

Диало́ги *Dialogues*

Listen to the conversations and answer the questions. Then listen again and repeat.

ДИАЛО́Г 1 *DIALOGUE 1*

08.02 *Sally goes with Ната́ша to visit Никола́й.*

1 How many children does Никола́й have?

Никола́й	Входи́те, Са́лли! Меня́ зову́т Никола́й.
Са́лли	Очень прия́тно, Никола́й.
Никола́й	Очень прия́тно, Са́лли. Сади́тесь, пожа́луйста.
Са́лли	(*sitting down on toy car*) Извини́те! Скажи́те, у вас есть семья́?
Никола́й	Да, есть. *(takes out his phone)* Посмотри́те. Э́то моя́ жена́, и вот де́ти, ви́дите? У меня́ сын и дочь. Их зову́т Алёша и Ли́за. Алёша о́чень ли́бит маши́ны и Ли́за лю́бит спорт. Алёша мой приёмный сын, но он мне как родной. Жена́ – учи́тельница. Её зову́т Га́ля. Жена́ и де́ти сейча́с на да́че.
Са́лли	На да́че? Как хорошо́. (*looking at next photo*) А кто э́то? Мать и оте́ц?
Никола́й	Да, э́то ма́ма и па́па. Они́ на пе́нсии, и ле́том они́ живу́т на да́че. Я их о́чень люблю́. А вот мой брат. Его́ зову́т Ви́ктор. Он студе́нт, хорошо́ говори́т по-неме́цки и по-англи́йски и хо́чет путеше́ствовать.
Са́лли	Интере́сно...
Николай	И вот моя́ сестра́. Её зову́т И́ра. Она́ о́чень энерги́чная де́вушка, игра́ет в баскетбо́л и лю́бит гуля́ть в дере́вне. И вот дя́дя и тётя. Они́ инжене́ры, рабо́тают на фа́брике в Новосиби́рске.

2 Read the conversation out loud and say it line by line.

08.03 Learn the parts of a house before going to the conversation! Listen as you read then listen again and repeat.

Улица Ми́ра	**óoleetsa Méera**	*street (of) peace*
у нас (есть)	**oo nas (yest')**	*we have*
гости́ная	**gastéenaya**	*living room*
спа́льня	**spál'nya**	*bedroom*
ку́хня	**kóokhnya**	*kitchen* (also *cookery*)
но́вый/ста́рый	**nóvy/stáry**	*new/old*
прекра́сный	**prikrásny**	*fine*
столо́вая	**stalóvaya**	*dining room*
на́ша соба́ка	**násha sabáka**	*our dog* (наш works like ваш)
кабине́т	**kabeenyét**	*study*
вид	**veet**	*view*
так прия́тно	**tak preeyátna**	*so pleasant*

ДИАЛО́Г 2 ***DIALOGUE 2***

08.04 *Серёжа, Tim and Бе́лла are comparing photos of their homes.*

1 Who lives in a flat and who lives in a house?

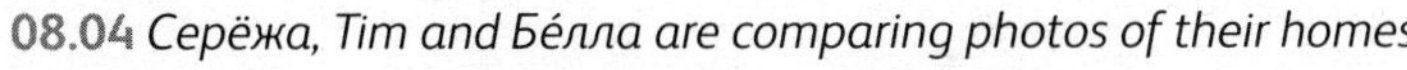

Серёжа	Я живу́ в кварти́ре на у́лице Ми́ра. У нас в кварти́ре гости́ная, спа́льня, ку́хня, ва́нная и балко́н. Кварти́ра но́вая, и у нас есть лифт и консье́рж. А где вы живёте, Тим?
Тим	Я живу́ в до́ме в Ливерпу́ле. Э́то ста́рый, большо́й дом. У нас больша́я гости́ная, прекра́сная столо́вая, ма́ленькая ку́хня, три спа́льни и ва́нная.
Серёжа	У вас есть сад?
Тим	Да, у нас большо́й сад. На́ша соба́ка, Три́кси, лю́бит там игра́ть.
Бе́лла	У меня́ ста́рая кварти́ра в до́ме на реке́ Мо́йке. Она́ краси́вая. У меня́ в кварти́ре гости́ная, кабине́т, ку́хня и ва́нная. У меня́ прекра́сный вид на ре́ку Мо́йку. Там так прия́тно!

2 **Now answer these questions about the first dialogue.**

a What family does Nikolai have?

b Where are they today?

c What does his brother do?

d What does his sister do?

e Where do his aunt and uncle work?

3 **Who lives where? Match the homes and people in the second dialogue. Put Бéлла, Серёжа, or Тим in the blank.**

a ____________ b ____________ c ____________

A дáча **dácha** (*country house*) can be a garden shed or a magnificent lodge. City dwellers often grow fruit, vegetables and flowers, gather berries and mushrooms in the woods, enjoy wild water swimming in rivers and lakes and visit at weekends to enjoy the fresh air and bring home-grown produce back to the city. Families may live there in warmer months.

Language discovery

1 У ВАС ЕСТЬ ...? *DO YOU HAVE ...?*

The question у́ вас есть? (lit. *by you is there?*) can be asked by raising intonation at the end of the phrase and eliciting the response Да, есть **Da, yest' ...** (*Yes, there is ...*), or in full, Да, у меня́ есть ... **Da, oo minyá yest' ...** (*Yes, by me there is ...*). To state what you have, simply omit the question mark: у́ вас есть брат *You have a brother*. у́ вас есть can be literally translated as *by you there is* and is used to express the notion of belonging. Look at the forms:

у меня́	**oo minyá**	*I have*	у нас	**oo nas**	*we have*
у тебя́	**oo tibyá**	*you have*	у вас	**oo vas**	*you have*
у него́	**oo nyivó**	*he/it has*	у ни́х	**oo neekh**	*they have*
у неё	**oo nyiyó**	*she has*			
у кого́?	**oo kavó**	*who has?*			

The word есть can add emphasis: У меня́ есть газе́та *I do have a newspaper*.

У меня́, у тебя́, etc. can mean *at my home*, *at your home*, or even *in my country* and is useful for comparing: У вас рождество́ седьмо́го января́, но у нас рождество́ два́дцать пя́того декабря́. *In your country Christmas is on 7 January, but in our country Christmas is on 25 December.*

2 MORE ABOUT VERBS

You already know that я хожу́ is used to say *I go somewhere* (habitually), and я иду́ is usually used to say *I am going somewhere* (now). Here are the verbs ходи́ть and идти́ in full. They both refer to going on foot, not by transport.

ходи́ть *to go habitually*		**идти́** *to go once*	
я хожу́	мы хо́дим	я иду́	мы идём
ты хо́дишь	вы хо́дите	ты идёшь	вы идёте
она́/оно́ хо́дит	они́ хо́дят	она́/оно́ идёт	они́ иду́т

Куда́ вы хо́дите ка́ждый день в 7 часо́в? *Where do you go every day at 7 o'clock?*

Куда́ вы идёте? *Where are you going now?*

3 POINTS OF THE COMPASS

The points of the compass are сéвер **syévyir** (*north*), юг **yook** (*south*), зáпад **zápat** (*west*), востóк **vastók** (*east*). To say *in the north,* etc., use на with the prepositional endings, adding -е to the end of the following word.

на сéвере **на зáпаде** **на востóке** **на юге** **в цéнтре**	**Áфрики, Áзии, Áнглии, Ирлáндии, Россúи, Уэ́льса, Шотлáндии** *of Africa, Asia, England, Ireland, Russia, Wales, Scotland*

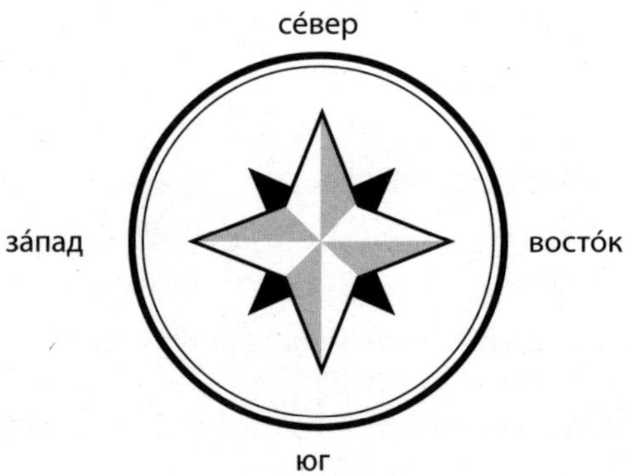

4 WHOSE IS IT?

The words for *your* (if you address someone as ты) and *our* are твой **tvoy** and наш **nash** respectively. Like мой (*my*) and ваш (*your*) (see Unit 4), they have different forms to agree with the gender of the nouns they refer to.

Masculine	Feminine	Neuter	Plural
твой сад	**твоя́** балала́йка	**твоё** пиани́но	**твои́** кни́ги
your garden	*your balalaika*	*your piano*	*your books*
наш сад	**на́ша** балала́йка	**на́ше** пиани́но	**на́ши** кни́ги
our garden	*our balalaika*	*our piano*	*our books*

The words егó **yivó** (*his*), её **yiyó** (*her*) and их **eekh** (*their*) are easier to use as they do not change. So, егó can be used with any noun to mean *his:* егó сад, егó балалáйка, егó пианúно, егó кнúги. Её (*her*) and их (*their*) are also simple.

5 *HIM, HER, THEM*: DIRECT OBJECT PRONOUNS

As well as meaning *his*, *her* and *their*, the words его́, её and их have another meaning: *him*, *her* and *them*, in phrases where people are the direct object of the verb. Look at the full range of *me*, *you*, *him*, *her*, *us*, *you*, *them*, many of which you have seen before, as in Как вас зову́т? (lit. *How you do they call?*)

ты лю́бишь меня́	*you love me*	вы лю́бите нас	*you love us*
я люблю́ тебя́	*I love you*	они́ лю́бят вас	*they love you*
она́ лю́бит его́	*she loves him*	мы лю́бим их	*we love them*
он лю́бит её	*he loves her*		

Practice

1 Look at these routes for St Petersburg's public transport. Which route (1, 2 or 3) should you take to go to the places below?

Route 1 Семна́дцатый тролле́йбус: Каза́нская пло́щадь –

Горо́ховая у́лица – Вите́бский вокза́л – За́городный проспе́кт – Моско́вский проспе́кт

Route 2 Шестьдеся́т тре́тий трамва́й: Финля́ндский вокза́л –

Сампсоние́вский мост – ста́нция метро́ 'Го́рьковская'

– Ту́чков мост

Route 3 Два́дцать восьмо́й авто́бус: Финля́ндский вокза́л –

Арсена́льная на́бережная – шоссе́ Револю́ции –

Индустриа́льный проспе́кт

a ________ Finland station
b ________ Arsenal Embankment
c ________ Revolution Highway
d ________ Moscow Avenue
e ________ Gor'kovskaya metro station
f ________ Tuchkov Bridge
g ________ Kazan Square
h ________ Industrial Avenue

2 08.05 **Listen to these descriptions of Ánya, Peter, Leoníd and Zoe. Note in English, information about the following points: where they live, where they work, their families, their hobbies, their goals.**

	А́ня	Пи́тер	Леони́д	Зо́я
живёт				
рабо́тает				
семья́				
хо́бби				
хо́чет				

3 08.06 **Complete the description of Nadyézhda's home and life with the words in the box. Listen to the recording and check your answers.**

> **лю́бит живёт её день**
> **магази́ны хо́дит ку́хня**

Наде́жда ________ в кварти́ре в Арха́нгельске, на се́вере Росси́и. У неё но́вая кварти́ра, не о́чень краси́вая, но Наде́жда лю́бит там жить потому́, что ________ недалеко́. В кварти́ре, у неё больша́я гости́ная и ма́ленькая спа́льня, ________ и ва́нная. Её муж рабо́тает в Москве́. В кварти́ре живу́т Наде́жда, её ма́ма и ________ дочь. Их зову́т Гали́на и Ма́ша. У них кот. Его́ зову́т Го́рби. Ма́ша его́ о́чень ________. Ка́ждый ________ Наде́жда хо́дит на фа́брику, где она́ рабо́тает. Ма́ша хо́дит в шко́лу, и ба́бушка ________ по магази́нам.

4 Read this property advert and list its features.

> Эли́тный ко́ттедж. Прести́жный райо́н. Электри́чество, вода́, газ. Джаку́зи и са́уна. Ками́н. Спу́тниковое ТВ. 250кв.м. Большо́й гара́ж.

____

____

____

5 Where are these cities? Put the correct compass direction in the blank.

сéвере юге востóке зáпаде

a Магадáн на ________ Россúи.
b Москвá на ________ Россúи.
c Иркýтск на ________ Россúи.
d Норúльск на ________ Россúи.

6 08.07 Listen to what each person has. Mark the correct column.

	Машúна	Брат	Кот	Квартúра	Дáча
Борúс					
Нáстя					
Лúза					

7 Choose the correct form of the verb to complete each sentence.

a Q: Скажúте, пожáлуйста. Где здесь банк?
A: Извинúте, я не знáете/знáю/знáем.

b Q: Кудá вы идý/идёшь/идёте?
A: Я идý/идёшь/идёте в музéй.

c Я хотúм/хóчешь/хочý купúть сувенúры.

d Он хорошó говорю́/говорúт/говоря́т по-рýсски.

e Где ты рабóтаем/рабóтают/рабóтаешь?

f Утром я зáвтракаю/зáвтракает/зáвтракаете в 7 часóв.

g Q: У вас есть хóбби?
A: Да, я óчень лю́бит/люблю́/лю́бят читáть.

h Мы игрáю/игрáет/игрáем в хоккéй.

i Онú ýжинает/ýжинают/ýжинаем пóздно вéчером.

Listen and understand

1 08.08 **Read the words as you listen and repeat.**

почему́?	**pachemóo?**	*why?*
потому́, что	**patamóo shta**	*because*
магази́н	**magazéen**	*shop*
по магази́нам	**pa magazéenam**	*round the shops*
наш го́род	**nash górat**	*our city*
истори́ческий	**eestaréecheskee**	*historical*
споко́йно	**spakóina**	*peaceful*
лес, в лесу́	**lyes, vlyesóo**	*forest, in the forest*
Приезжа́йте к нам в го́сти	**Preeyezháitye k nam v góstee**	*Come and visit us as a guest* (lit. *Come to us as guest*)

ДИАЛОГ 3 ***DIALOGUE 3***

2 08.09 **You're conducting interviews. Listen as you ask people why they have chosen to live in the city or country.**

Вы	Почему́ вы лю́бите жить в го́роде?
А́нна	Я люблю́ жить в го́роде потому́, что мо́жно ходи́ть на конце́рты, в теа́тр, в кино́, по магази́нам. Наш го́род истори́ческий, краси́вый. Мы живём в це́нтре и у нас есть ста́нция метро́ недалеко́.
Вы	Са́ша, почему́ вы лю́бите жить в дере́вне?
Са́ша	Я люблю́ жить в дере́вне потому́, что там споко́йно и мо́жно гуля́ть в лесу́. Приезжа́йте к нам в го́сти. В дере́вне о́чень прия́тно.

3 Listen again and complete the missing information.

Я люблю́ жить в го́роде потому́, что мо́жно ходи́ть на конце́рты, _______, в кино́, ________ ________. Наш го́род истори́ческий, ________. Мы живём в це́нтре и у нас есть ста́нция метро́ недалеко́.

Test yourself

1 Choose the correct answer.

a If someone had a журнал, would they (eat it/read it/put it in a letter box)?

b ГУМ is in the city of (St Petersburg/Magadan/Moscow).

c If you were at a вокза́л, would you catch (a train/a plane/a cold)?

d If you were speaking to an официа́нт, would you be (showing your passport/ordering a drink/paying a fine)?

e Is ка́ша (porridge/someone's name/a cash desk)?

f Is пра́здник (a day of the week/a shop assistant/a holiday)?

g If you are walking along a на́бережная, should you look out for (a runway/a river/a hospital)?

h If someone asked you Ско́лько сейча́с вре́мени? would you answer with (your name/the time/how much something costs)?

i If someone told you that the date today was девятна́дцатое а́вгуста, would you think that it was (20th August/9th August/19th August)?

j If someone said to you Встре́тимся в пя́тницу, would you expect to meet them on (Friday/Sunday/Monday)?

SELF CHECK

	I CAN. . .
○	. . . talk about home and family (yours and theirs!).
○	. . . be a good guest in a Russian home.
○	. . . plan a route on public transport.

9

In this unit, you will learn how to:

» shop for souvenirs.
» shop for food.
» use ‘can’ and ‘may’.
» talk about quantities.

Где мóжно купи́ть самовáр?

My progress tracker

DAY / DATE

Souvenirs

When shopping for сувени́ры (*souvenirs*) in Russia, one favorite is the самовáр (*samovar*), a traditional urn, usually powered by charcoal or electricity, in which water is heated to make tea. Very strong tea is made in a tiny teapot which stands on top of the samovar to keep warm. A little is poured into a glass, topped with water from the samovar, and is taken with сáхар (*sugar*), лимóн (*lemon*) or варéнье (*fruit preserves*). Of course, these days most people use a kettle, mug and teabag! Other popular souvenirs include the балалáйка (*balalaika*), the triangular-stringed musical instrument used for playing Russian folk music, and the матрёшка (*matryoshka doll*) which is made of wood, brightly painted, and contains a whole series of smaller dolls hidden inside each other. There are also beautiful wooden painted boxes in the Палéх (**Palyékh**) or Хохломá (**Khokhlomá**) style, крýжево (*lace*) and shawls, as well as books of photos альбóмы (*albums*).

What do you think this is? чай с сáхаром и с лимóном.

Vocabulary builder

09.01 Listen as you look at the words, then listen again and try to imitate the speakers.

ХОДИ́ТЬ ПО МАГАЗИ́НАМ ***GOING ROUND THE SHOPS***

Универма́г *Department store*

пода́рок/пода́рки	*present/s*
оде́жда	*clothes*
ша́пка	*fur hat*

Сувени́ры *Souvenirs*

электри́ческий самова́р	*electric samovar*
плато́к/платки́	*shawl/s*
деревя́нная игру́шка	*wooden toy*
икра́	*caviar*

Кио́ск *Kiosk*

газе́та	*newspaper*
журна́л	*magazine*
план	*plan*
ка́рта	*map*
откры́тка	*postcard*
моро́женое	*ice cream*

Апте́ка *Chemist's*

аспири́н	*aspirin*
лека́рство	*medicine*

Can you figure out which of these are not grocery items? Mark them off the list:

цветы́	пи́во	хлеб	зелёный чай
минера́льная вода́	газе́та	пи́цца	джи́нсы

Диало́ги *Dialogues*

Listen to the conversations and answer the questions. Then listen again and repeat.

ДИАЛО́Г 1 *DIALOGUE 1*

09.02 *Chris is asking Olég to help organize her day.*

1 What does Chris want to do today?

Крис	Я сего́дня хочу́ ходи́ть по магази́нам.
Оле́г	Что ты хо́чешь купи́ть?
Крис	Пода́рки и сувени́ры. Я хочу́ купи́ть кни́ги, деревя́нные игру́шки, откры́тки и самова́р. Я о́чень люблю́ ру́сский чай с лимо́ном.
Оле́г	Поня́тно. Кни́ги и откры́тки продаю́тся в магази́не 'Дом Кни́ги'. Э́то недалеко́.
Крис	А где продаю́тся самова́ры и игру́шки?
Оле́г	В магази́не 'Ру́сский сувени́р'. Кото́рый сейча́с час?
Крис	Де́вять часо́в.
Оле́г	Хорошо́. 'Дом Кни́ги' открыва́ется в де́вять часо́в.
Крис	Как попа́сть в 'Дом Кни́ги'?
Оле́г	Три остано́вки на авто́бусе. Остано́вка там, напро́тив.

	Later, in 'Ру́сский сувени́р'
Продавщи́ца	Вам помо́чь?
Крис	Пожа́луйста, да! Покажи́те, пожа́луйста, э́тот самова́р. Нет, вот э́тот. Оле́г, како́й краси́вый самова́р! Де́вушка, э́то электри́ческий самова́р?
Продавщи́ца	Да, электри́ческий. Отку́да вы?
Крис	Я англича́нка, живу́ в Ло́ндоне.
Продавщи́ца	Не волну́йтесь. Моя́ тётя живёт в Ло́ндоне, и она́ говори́т, что на́ши самова́ры там хорошо́ рабо́тают.
Крис	Поня́тно. Покажи́те, пожа́луйста, э́ти деревя́нные игру́шки. Да, кра́сные и зелёные. И вот э́ти жёлтые.
Продавщи́ца	Вот э́ти?
Крис	Да. Спаси́бо. Напиши́те, пожа́луйста, ско́лько они́ сто́ят.

2 Answer the questions.

a What time is it when Chris starts to plan her day?
b What four things does she want to buy?
c Is it far to the bookstore?
d Where is the bus stop?
e What is the Russian for *she says that*?
f How does Chris know that the samovar will work in England?
g What colors are the toys she wants to look at?

3 Complete the missing words from the conversation in Russian.

a ________. 'Дом Кни́ги' открыва́ется в де́вять часо́в.
b Q: ________ ________?
A: ________. Спаси́бо. Напиши́те, ________, ско́лько они́ сто́ят.

4 Listen again and repeat one line at a time.

5 Now make up your own dialogue. Buy things you would particularly like.

ДИАЛО́Г 2 *DIALOGUE 2*

09.03 *Nick is going shopping at the dairy section of the market.*

1 What is he shopping for?

Продавщи́ца	Слу́шаю вас.
Ник	У вас есть сыр?
Продавщи́ца	Есть ли у нас сыр? Да, коне́чно. Вот он.
Ник	Како́й э́то сыр? Мо́жно посмотре́ть, пожа́луйста?
Продавщи́ца	Мо́жно. Э́то эсто́нский сыр. Сто́ит две́сти рубле́й кило́.
Ник	Повтори́те, пожа́луйста, ме́дленнее.
Продавщи́ца	Две́сти рубле́й.
Ник	Э́то до́рого?
Продавщи́ца	Нет, недо́рого. Ско́лько вы хоти́те?
Ник	Пятьсо́т грамм. Ско́лько с меня́?
Продавщи́ца	Сто рубле́й. Всё?
Ник	Да, всё. Где плати́ть?
Продавщи́ца	В ка́ссу.
Ник	А где ка́сса?
Продавщи́ца	Здесь.
Ник	Да. Спаси́бо. Како́й здесь отде́л?
Продавщи́ца	Сырный.

2 Find the Russian in the conversation that means:

- **a** Could I have a look?
- **b** How much do you want?
- **c** Is that all?
- **d** here
- **e** department
- **f** How much do I owe?

3 Now put yourself in Nick's place and work through the dialogue covering up his lines and saying his part. Don't try to understand every word but try to get the gist.

Language discovery

Go back to the two dialogues and find the phrases that mean:

- **a** understood
- **b** it's not far
- **c** What time is it?
- **d** good
- **e** May I help you?
- **f** Where are you from?
- **g** don't worry
- **h** yes, of course
- **i** Repeat, please; more slowly.

1 WHAT'S IT CALLED?

When shopping for anything, it helps to speak the language! Study the grocery vocabulary.

09.04 Суперма́ркет *Supermarket*

гастроно́м	*grocer's*
Здесь продаю́тся ...	*Here you can buy ...*
проду́кты	*groceries*
мя́со	*meat*
ры́ба	*fish*
колбаса́	*sausage (salami)*
соси́ска	*sausage (frankfurter)*
ко́фе, чай, са́хар	*coffee, tea, sugar*
конфе́ты	*sweets*
торт	*cake*
вино́, пи́во, во́дка	*wine, beer, vodka*
моло́чные проду́кты	*dairy produce*
молоко́	*milk*
смета́на	*sour cream*
сыр	*cheese*
ма́сло	*butter*

Бу́лочная *Bakery*

чёрный/бе́лый хлеб	*black/white bread*
бато́н	*long loaf*
бу́лка	*sweet bread roll*
су́шка	*dry ring-shaped biscuit*

Ры́нок *Market*

све́жие фру́кты/о́вощи/цветы́	*fresh fruit/vegetables/flowers*
я́блоко/я́блоки	*apple/s*
гру́ша	*pear*
апельси́н	*orange*
карто́шка	*potato*
помидо́р	*tomato*
огуре́ц/огурцы́	*cucumber/s*

2 СКО́ЛЬКО ВЫ ХОТИ́ТЕ? *HOW MUCH DO YOU WANT?*

After any expression of quantity (kilo, liter, packet, etc.) the next word will change its ending to the genitive: кило́ бана́нов *a kilo of bananas*.

кило́	*kilo*	ба́нка	*jar, tin*
грамм	*gram*	буты́лка	*bottle*
литр	*liter*	па́чка	*packet*
метр	*meter*	сто грамм/ пятьсо́т грамм	*100 grams/* *500 grams*

3 WHERE DO YOU GO?

Here is an alphabetical list of types of shops in a major Russian city, and of items to buy. Many words will be familiar, and the rest you should probably be able to work out. What are the English translations of the words below?

Автомоби́ли	Музыка́льные инструме́нты
Антиквариа́т	Мя́со
Аудио-Видеоте́хника	О́вощи-фру́кты
Бу́лочная	О́птика
Гастроно́м	Пода́рки
Диети́ческие проду́кты	Ры́ба
Диза́йн-сту́дия	Спорти́вные това́ры
Кни́ги	Сувени́ры
Колбаса́	Таба́к
Косме́тика	Цветы́
Моло́чные проду́кты	Часы́

4 HOW DO I SAY IT?

09.05 Listen to what to say to a shop assistant and what they might reply.

What you say:

Мо́жно посмотре́ть? — *May I have a look?*

Покажи́те, да́йте ... — *Show me, give me ...*

Ско́лько сто́ит? Ско́лько сто́ят? — *How much is it? How much are they?*

Напиши́те, пожа́луйста, ско́лько сто́ит. — *Please write down how much it is.*

Повтори́те, пожа́луйста, ме́дленнее. — *Repeat that more slowly, please.*

У вас есть/Есть ли у вас кни́ги о спо́рте? — *Do you have any books about sport?*

Пожа́луйста, да. — *Yes, please.*

Спаси́бо, нет. — *No, thank you.*

Ско́лько с меня́? — *How much do I owe?*

До́рого/Недо́рого. — *That's expensive/not expensive.*

Всё? Да, всё. — *Is that all? Yes, that's all.*

Где плати́ть? В ка́ссу? — *Where do I pay? At the cash desk?*

Где ка́сса? — *Where is the cash desk?*

Напро́тив — *opposite*

Сто два́дцать рубле́й — *120 roubles*

Магази́н откры́т/закры́т. — *The shop is open/closed.*

Я хочу́ купи́ть ... — *I want to buy ...*

Куда́ мне пойти́? — *Where should I go?*

Где продаю́тся газе́ты? — *Where are newspapers sold?*

What the shop assistant says:

Слу́шаю вас. — *I'm listening. (May I help?)*

Вам помо́чь? — *May I help you?*

Что вы хоти́те? — *What do you want?*

Ско́лько вы хоти́те? — *How much do you want?*

Сыр сто́ит 200 рубле́й килогра́мм. — *Cheese costs 200 roubles a kilo.*

Practice

1 Look at the sign. What does the shop sell?

2 Read this list of products at a supermarket and answer the questions.

Майоне́з

Сыр Га́уда, Голла́ндия

Киви́, Гре́ция

Лимо́ны, Испа́ния

Мандари́ны, Испа́ния

Ке́тчуп, Болга́рия

Чай инди́йский

Ко́фе, Брази́лия

Шокола́д, Герма́ния

Во́дка, 'Столи́чная', 'Сми́рнофф', 'А́бсолют'

- **a** Which two fruits from Spain can you buy?
- **b** What sort of cheese is there?
- **c** What has been imported from Bulgaria?
- **d** What sort of tea can you buy?
- **e** Which brands of vodka are listed?

3 09.06 **You are in a grocer's. Listen to people asking for things. Choose the items requested on the list.**

чай	сахар
огурец	колбаса
сосиски	конфеты
банка кофе	торт
кило помидоров	мясо
рыба	бутылка пива

4 **Find five drinks and six types of food below.**

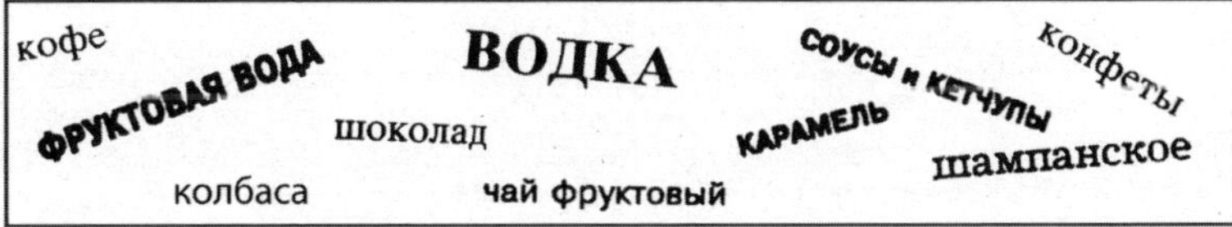

5 **Ask in the гастроно́м if they have:**

a salami sausage
b tea
c cake
d fish
e milk
f oranges
g cucumbers

6 09.07 **Listen to three conversations. Note in Russian or English what Sásha wants to buy, the shop he needs and the directions he is given.**

Са́ша хо́чет купи́ть ...	Магази́н	Куда́?
a		
b		
c		

Go further

Try it!

Here is a tongue twister for you to learn by heart to practice the letters с and ш. It means *Sásha walked along the road and sucked a biscuit* (lit. *walked Sásha along road and sucked biscuit*).

Шла Са́ша по шоссе́ и соса́ла су́шку.

You have met the expression Мо́жно? (*May I?*) Мо́жно (*You may*). The opposite of this is Нельзя́ (*It is forbidden*). Во всех обще́ственных места́х нельзя́ кури́ть means *In public places it is forbidden to smoke.* Sometimes this may be put more simply as Не кури́ть.

Test yourself

1 Look at these questions. What does the shop assistant mean?

a Слу́шаю вас.

b Вам помо́чь?

c Ско́лько вы хоти́те?

d Вот э́ти?

2 How would you say these phrases in Russian? Say your answers out loud.

a Can I have a look?

b Show me.

c How much is it?

d Do you have sweets?

e That's expensive.

f Repeat that please.

SELF CHECK

	I CAN...
○	... shop for souvenirs.
○	... shop for food.
○	... use 'can' and 'may'.
○	... talk about quantities.

10

In this unit, you will learn how to:

» talk about the weather.
» talk about the past and future.
» understand tourist information online.
» book an excursion.

Какáя сегóдня погóда?

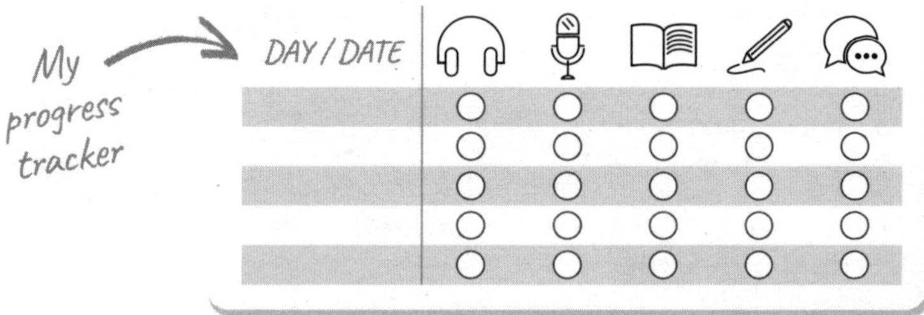

On holiday

Popular destinations for Russian holidaymakers include Еги́пет (*Egypt*), Таилáнд (*Thailand*), Тýрция (*Turkey*), the ОАЭ (*UAE/United Arab Emirates*), Сейшельские острова (the Seychelles), Мальдивы (the Maldives), Танзания (Tanzania), Абхазия (Abkhazia). You may hear a different word for holiday if you talk to schoolchildren and students: кани́кулы. Here is a typical advert for a holiday.

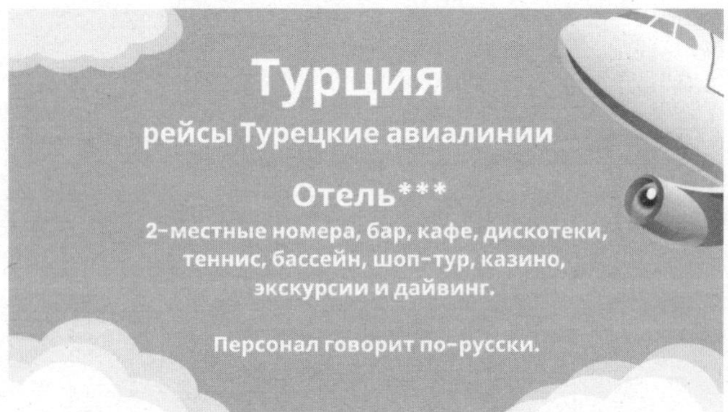

Does the hotel in the advert offer a spa and exercise room as part of its amenities?

Vocabulary builder

10.01 Listen as you look at the words, then listen again and try to imitate the speakers.

NEW EXPRESSIONS

Какáя сегóдня погóда?	*What's the weather like today?*
Сегóдня хóлодно.	*Today it's cold.*
Прохлáдно.	*It's cool.*
Теплó.	*It's warm.*
Слúшком жáрко.	*It's too hot.*
Дýшно.	*It's close.*
Вéтрено.	*It's windy.*
Тумáнно.	*It's foggy.*
Пáсмурно.	*It's overcast.*
Идёт дождь.	*It's raining.*
Идёт снег.	*It's snowing.*
Сóлнце свéтит.	*The sun is shining.*
Морóз.	*It's frosty.*
температýра вóздуха	*air temperature*
температýра воды́	*water temperature*
плюс 5 грáдусов	*5 degrees (Celsius)*
мúнус одúн грáдус	*– 1 (Celsius)*
Вéтер юго-зáпадный.	*The wind is south-westerly.*
Какóй прогнóз погóды на зáвтра?	*What is the weather forecast for tomorrow?*
Зáвтра бýдет хóлодно/теплó.	*Tomorrow it will be cold/warm.*
Зáвтра бýдет дождь/снег.	*Tomorrow there will be rain/snow.*
веснá, лéто, óсень, зимá	*spring, summer, autumn, winter*
зúмний спорт	*winter sport*
Какóе твоё любúмое врéмя гóда?	*Which is your favorite season?*
Моё любúмое врéмя гóда – веснá.	*My favorite season is spring.*
Что дéлать?	*What is to be done?*

Диало́ги *Dialogues*

Listen to the conversations and answer the questions. Then listen again and repeat.

ДИАЛО́Г 1 *DIALOGUE 1*

10.02 *Rosemary is spending her first winter in Russia and is determined to make the most of the snow. Her friend Maxím is not so keen.*

1 What does Rosemary want to do today?

Ро́узмэри	Макси́м, ты хо́чешь сего́дня ката́ться на лы́жах в лесу́?
Макси́м	Нет, не о́чень хочу́. Сего́дня хо́лодно.
Ро́узмэри	Коне́чно хо́лодно! Зима́! Но сего́дня так прекра́сно. Моро́з и со́лнце све́тит.
Макси́м	Да, но по ра́дио говоря́т, что температу́ра во́здуха сего́дня ми́нус де́сять гра́дусов. Сли́шком хо́лодно. Я хочу́ смотре́ть телеви́зор и чита́ть до́ма, где тепло́.
Ро́узмэри	Смотре́ть телеви́зор? Макси́м, что ты! Как э́то мо́жет быть? Ты совсе́м не лю́бишь зи́му?
Макси́м	Нет, я люблю́ ле́то, когда́ жа́рко. Мо́жно гуля́ть на пля́же и есть моро́женое.
Ро́узмэри	Поня́тно. Я то́же о́чень люблю́ ле́то. Но я так хочу́ сего́дня ката́ться на лы́жах. Жаль. Что де́лать?
Макси́м	Мо́жно позвони́ть А́ндрю. Он о́чень лю́бит зи́мний спорт.
Ро́узмэри	Пра́вильно. На́до позвони́ть А́ндрю. Како́й у него но́мер телефо́на?
Макси́м	Семьсо́т три́дцать де́вять, пятна́дцать, со́рок два.

2 Now answer these questions.

a What is the weather like?
b What does Maxím want to do?
c What is his favorite season and why?
d What does Rosemary decide to do?
e What is Andrew's phone number?

10.03 Learn these *freetime* expressions before going to the next conversation!

де́лать **(1)**	*to do*
свобо́дное вре́мя	*free time*
лови́ть **(2)** ры́бу (я ловлю́, ты ло́вишь)	*to go fishing*
собира́ть **(1)** ма́рки, грибы́	*to collect stamps, mushrooms*
гото́вить **(2)** (я гото́влю, ты гото́вишь)	*to cook*
ката́ться на лы́жах, на конька́х, на са́нках	*to ski, skate, sledge*
ката́ться на велосипе́де, на ло́шади, на ло́дке	*to cycle, ride a horse, go boating*
отдыха́ть **(1)** за грани́цей, на берегу́ мо́ря	*to holiday abroad, at the seaside*
купа́ться в мо́ре	*to swim in the sea*
загора́ть **(1)** на пля́же	*to sunbathe on the beach*
гуля́ть **(1)** в лесу́	*to walk in the woods*
ходи́ть **(2)** в теа́тр, кино́ (я хожу́, ты хо́дишь)	*to go to the theater, cinema*
ходи́ть **(2)** по магази́нам	*to go shopping*
игра́ть **(1)** в футбо́л, в ша́хматы	*to play football, chess*
игра́ть **(1)** на гита́ре	*to play the guitar*
рисова́ть **(1)** (я рису́ю, ты рису́ешь)	*to draw*
танцева́ть **(1)** (я танцу́ю, ты танцу́ешь)	*to dance*
акти́вный челове́к	*active person*
обы́чно	*usually*
ча́сто	*often*
с удово́льствием	*with pleasure*
идёт бале́т, о́пера, фильм, пье́са.	*There is a ballet, an opera, a film, a play on.*
Ты хо́чешь пойти́ в/на ... ?	*Do you want to go to ... ?*

ДИАЛО́Г 2 *DIALOGUE 2*

10.04 *Helen and Yúra are talking about their hobbies. They seem to have very different ideas about how to spend their free time but they are able to agree on going somewhere together tomorrow.*

1 Where do they decide to go?

Хе́лен	Каки́е у тебя́ хо́бби?
Ю́ра	Я о́чень акти́вный челове́к. Зимо́й я люблю́ игра́ть в хокке́й и ката́ться на лы́жах, а ле́том я ча́сто гуля́ю в дере́вне и игра́ю в те́ннис. Я то́же люблю́ купа́ться в мо́ре. О́сенью я собира́ю грибы́ в лесу́. А у тебя́ есть хо́бби?
Хе́лен	Да, но я не о́чень акти́вный челове́к. Я люблю́ слу́шать ра́дио, игра́ть в ша́хматы, чита́ть кни́ги, смотре́ть фи́льмы и ходи́ть на конце́рты.
Ю́ра	В Ланка́стре есть теа́тр?
Хе́лен	Коне́чно есть. Но я не о́чень ча́сто хожу́ в театр в Ланка́стре потому́, что до́рого сто́ит.
Ю́ра	Да, поня́тно. Здесь в Краснода́ре у нас хоро́шие теа́тры. Ты хо́чешь пойти́ в теа́тр за́втра ве́чером?
Хе́лен	Да, с удово́льствием!

2 Find out where Helen and Yúra are from and what their interests are.

3 Look at the icons and identify the activities you can do at a resort on the shores of the Чёрное мо́ре (*Black Sea*). Begin: Здесь мо́жно ...

Language discovery

Compare: бу́дет хо́лодно, тепло́ (future) with Сего́дня хо́лодно (present). What shows future tense in Russian?

1 TALKING ABOUT THE FUTURE

For most expressions, simply start the phrase with бу́дет (*there will be*), so to say *it will be sunny*: бу́дет со́лнечно or со́лнце бу́дет све́тить (*the sun will shine*).

2 TALKING ABOUT THE PAST

Remove the last two letters from most verbs, add –л for singular and masculine, -ла for singular and feminine and -ли for plural.

3 TALKING ABOUT THE FUTURE AND PAST WITH *TO BE*

There is no real verb *to be* in the present tense, but there is one in the future and past tenses. The infinitive of the verb is быть and this is how it works. To say *I will be in Moscow on Thursday*: Я бу́ду в Москве́ в четве́рг.

The future with *to be*

я бу́ду	*I will be*	мы бу́дем	*we will be*
ты бу́дешь	*you will be*	вы бу́дете	*you will be*
он/она́/оно́ бу́дет	*he/she/it will be*	они́ бу́дут	*they will be*

The past with *to be*

я был	*I was* (m)	я была́	*I was* (f)
ты был	*you were* (m)	ты была́	*you were* (f)
он был	*he was* (m)	она́ была́	*she was* (f)
мы бы́ли	*we were*		
вы бы́ли	*you were* (pl)		
они́ бы́ли	*they were*		

For a man, *I was in Moscow on Saturday* is я был в Москве́ в суббо́ту.

4 TALKING ABOUT CONDITIONALS: *IF … I WOULD HAVE …*

To talk about past conditional situations – for example, *If I had been in Moscow on Saturday, I would have gone shopping* – the condition or if phrase begins with е́сли бы … , as in е́сли бы я была́ в Москве́ в суббо́ту, я бы ходи́ла по магази́нам for a female speaker.

Practice

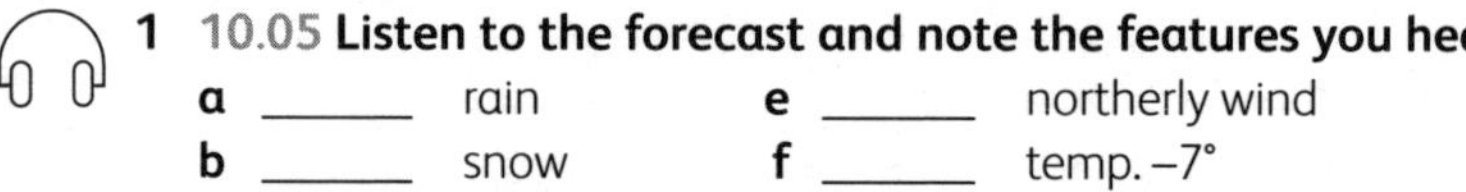

1 10.05 **Listen to the forecast and note the features you hear.**

a	______	rain	**e**	______	northerly wind
b	______	snow	**f**	______	temp. –7°
c	______	warm	**g**	______	frost
d	______	cold	**h**	______	sun

2 Give today's weather in Russia. You can check your answers against suggestions in the back of the book. Don't forget to say *in the north* на се́вере, *in the south* на ю́ге, *in the west* на за́паде, *in the east* на восто́ке.

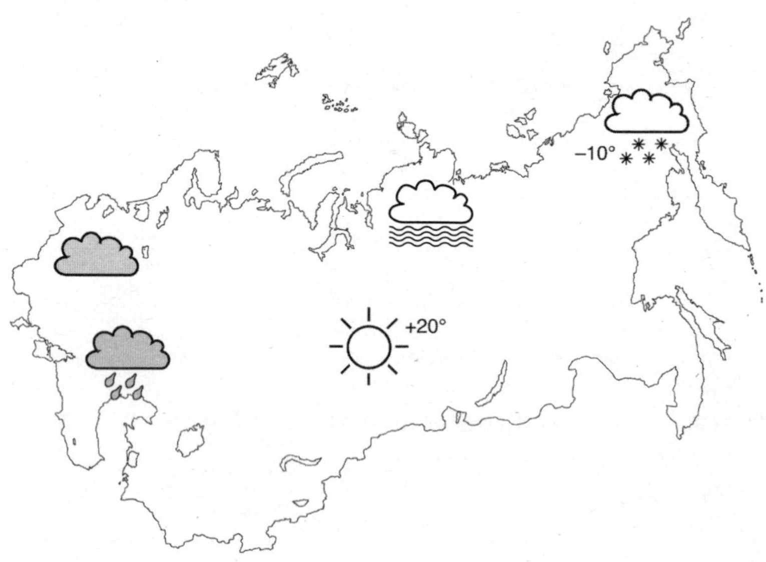

3 **Match the captions to the pictures of the weather.**

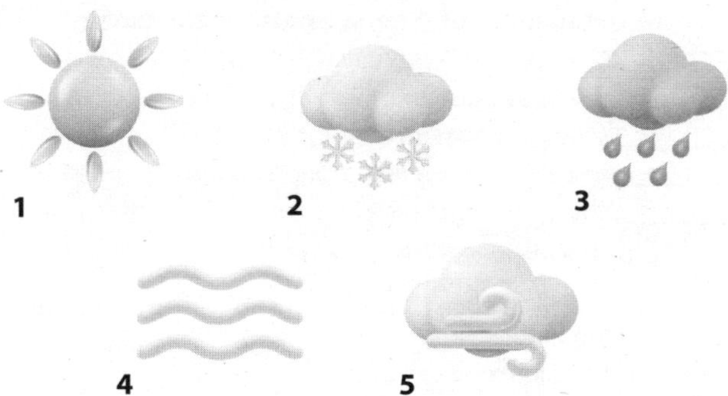

a идёт дождь

b тума́нно

c идёт снег

d ве́трено

e со́лнце све́тит

4 10.06 **Listen to the mini dialogues, then match the dialogues and titles: (1) At the kiosk (2) An invitation to the theater (3) At the theater.**

a ______________________

Де́вушка	Ва́ши биле́ты, пожа́луйста.
Ва́ня	Одну́ мину́точку. Вот они́.
Де́вушка	Хоти́те програ́мму?
Ва́ня	Да. Да́йте, пожа́луйста, три програ́ммы.

b ______________________

Ла́ра	Скажи́те, пожа́луйста, когда́ идёт бале́т 'Жизе́ль'?
Киоскёр	Восьмо́го, девя́того и деся́того апре́ля.

c ______________________

Га́ля	У меня́ есть биле́ты в Большо́й теа́тр. Вы свобо́дны?
Чарльс	Коне́чно. Как хорошо́! Биле́ты на сего́дня?
Га́ля	Да, на сего́дня на ве́чер.
Чарльс	Где мы встре́тимся?
Га́ля	У меня́ в кварти́ре в ше́сть часо́в.

5 Whatever Líza suggests, you use the weather as an excuse not to do it. Give the number of a good excuse in the blank.

a ________ Хóчешь пойти́ на пляж?
b ________ Хóчешь покатáться на велосипéде?
c ________ Хóчешь пойти́ на концéрт?
d ________ Хóчешь пойти́ в лес собирáть грибы́?
e ________ Хóчешь покатáться на конькáх?
f ________ Хóчешь искупáться в мóре?
g ________ Хóчешь пойти́ на стадиóн на футбóл?

1 Нет, сегóдня идёт дождь.
2 Нет, сегóдня сли́шком хóлодно.
3 Нет, сегóдня сли́шком жáрко.
4 Нет, сегóдня тумáнно.
5 Нет, сегóдня вéтрено.
6 Нет, сегóдня дýшно.
7 Нет, сегóдня сóлнце свéтит.

6 Read this message from Арина to Лена and answer the questions.

a Where is she staying?
b What is the weather like?
c What does she do every day?

Здравствуй, Лена. Мы отдыхаем в Сочи и живём в гостинице на берегу моря. Солнце светит и сейчас жарко. Каждый день я ем мороженое и играю в волейбол на пляже. Арина.

7 Where would you like to go if you could go anywhere? Describe your ideal holiday in Russian. Include a description of the place with its amenities or facilities, the weather and the activities you would like to do there.

Go further

When talking to Russians socially you may find it helpful to ask open questions, such as *What do you like to do in your free time?* Что вы любите делать де́лаете в свобо́дное вре́мя? You can listen and learn while the conversation flows. You may also find out about interesting activities, such as swimming in rivers and lakes in winter in holes cut in to the ice.

Answer these questions about your favorite things.

a Како́е твоё люби́мое вре́мя го́да?
b Како́й твой люби́мый спорт?
c Кака́я твоя́ люби́мая кни́га?
d Кака́я твоя́ люби́мая ма́рка маши́ны?
e Каки́е твои́ люби́мые фи́льмы?
f Каки́е твои́ люби́мые компози́торы/спортсме́ны?

НА УЛИЦЕ, ПО́ЗДНО.	LATE AT NIGHT, ON THE STREET.
– Куда́ ты идёшь так по́здно?	– Hey, where are you headed this late?
– Пора́ идти́ домо́й.	– It's time to go home.
– Почему́ так ра́но?	– What, already? (Why so early?)

Test yourself

1 What do these phrases mean?

- **a** Какáя сегóдня погóда?
- **b** Какóе твоё люби́мое врéмя гóда?
- **c** Что ты любишь делать в свобóдное врéмя?
- **d** Идёт дóждь.
- **e** Ты хóчешь пойти́ в кинó?

2 How would you say the following in Russian? Say your answers out loud.

- **a** with pleasure
- **b** I like to watch films.
- **c** Today it's too hot.
- **d** Can I book an excursion?
- **e** No, I don't really want to.
- **f** Tomorrow there will be rain.

SELF CHECK

	I CAN. . .
○	. . . talk about the weather.
○	. . . talk about the past and future.
○	. . . understand tourist information online.
○	. . . talk about holiday activities.
○	. . . describe locations.

Review 3

1 What are these dates? Choose the correct answer.

a вто́рник восьмо́е апре́ля
 1 Tuesday 8th of April
 2 Wednesday 19th of March

b четве́рг два́дцать пе́рвое ию́ня
 1 Thursday 21st of June
 2 Tuesday 21st of July

c воскресе́нье двена́дцатое ноября́
 1 Saturday 22nd of January
 2 Sunday 12th of November

d суббо́та пе́рвое ма́я
 1 Saturday 1st of May
 2 Monday 10th of March

e среда́ девятна́дцатая февраля́
 1 Tuesday 29th of December
 2 Wednesday 19th of February

Points: _______ / 5

2 Choose the correct form of the word to complete the sentences. Then put the sentences in English.

a Я (живу́/живёт/живу́т) в Москве.
b У меня́ дочь. (Её/Его́/Их) зову́т Ната́ша.
c Они́ (рабо́тает/рабо́таем/рабо́тают) на фа́брике.

Points: _______ / 6

3 Say these phrases in Russian.

a Where do you live?
b Where do you work?
c Do you have any hobbies? (formal)
d Do you like sport?
e I have a dog.
f Do you have a brother? (informal)
g They have a big apartment.
h Is this her passport?

i Does she love her?
j He speaks Russian well.

Points: _______ / 10

4 What is the Russian for these family-member terms?

a father
b mother
c husband
d wife
e son
f daughter
g brother
h sister
i aunt
j uncle
k grandfather
l grandmother

Points: _______ /6

5 These phrases can be used as instructions. What do they mean?

a Покажи́те
b Повтори́те
c Напиши́те
d Не волну́йтесь
e Ме́дленнее
f Да́йте

Points: _______ / 6

6 You are in a shop. How would you say the following?

a Can I have a look?
b How much is it?
c That's expensive.
d May I?
e That's all, thank you.
f Do you have black bread?

Points: _______ / 6

7 What is the shop assistant saying to you? Give the English for these sentences.

a Слу́шаю вас.
b Всё?
c Вам помо́чь?

d Ско́лько вы хоти́те?
e Поня́тно.
f Здесь продаю́тся фру́кты и о́вощи.
g Что вы хоти́те?
h Эти конфе́ты сто́ят три́ста се́мьдесят рубле́й.
i Каки́е?
j Коне́чно.

Points: _______ /10

8 What is the weather like? Choose the correct answer.

a Сего́дня хо́лодно и ве́трено. Идёт дождь.
  1 Today it's cold and cloudy. It's raining.
  2 Today it's cold and windy. It's raining.
b Сего́дня сли́шком жа́рко. Плюс три́дцать гра́дусов и ду́шно.
  1 Today it's beautiful. It's clear and sunny.
  2 Today it's too hot. It's 30 degrees and close.
c За́втра бу́дет снег и моро́з.
  1 Tomorrow there will be snow and frost.
  2 Tomorrow there will not be snow or frost.

Points: _______ /3

9 What do these people like? Choose the best answer.

a Я о́чень люблю́ зи́му. Я люблю́ ката́ться на лы́жах в лесу́.
  1 Winter, skiing in the forest.
  2 Winter, skating on lakes.
b Я люблю́ о́сень, когда́ мо́жно собира́ть грибы́.
  1 Autumn, watching leaves fall.
  2 Autumn, collecting mushrooms.
c Ле́том я люблю́ отдыха́ть за грани́цей, загора́ть на пля́же и купа́ться в мо́ре.
  1 Summer, holidays abroad, sunbathing on the beach, swimming in the sea.
  2 Summer, going abroad, sunbathing on the beach and swimming.
d Весно́й я люблю́ ката́ться на велосипе́де. Со́лнце све́тит но прохла́дно.
  1 Spring, riding a bicycle. Sunny warm weather.
  2 Spring, riding a bicycle. Sunny but cool.

Points: _______ /4

10 How would you say these phrases in Russian?

a I really don't like to watch television.
b What do you do in your spare time? (formal)
c In the summer I will be in Moscow.
d Do you want to go to the park tomorrow morning? (informal)

Points: _______ /4

Total points: _______ /60

Answer key

INTRODUCTION TO RUSSIAN

Part 1: The Russian alphabet

1 a2, b4, c1, d5, e3
2 a3, b4, c2, d5, e1
3 a3, b1, c2
4 a2, b1, c4, d3
5 те́ннис – tennis (image c), сну́кер – snooker (image a), стадио́н – stadium (image d), кри́кет – cricket (image b)
a5, b2, c4, d1, e7, f3, g6
6 a6, b1, c8, d7, e3, f4, g9, h5, i2
7 a4, b3, c2, d1
8 a3, b7, c8, d9, e5, f1, g4, h6, i2
9 Ivan, <u>Nina</u>, Alexander, Vladimir, <u>Ekaterina</u>, <u>Liza</u>, Lev, <u>Irina</u>, Valentin, <u>Larisa</u>
10 а́том – atom, коме́та – comet, метео́р – meteor, кли́мат – climate, механи́зм – mechanism, микроско́п – microscope, микроб – microbe, кило́ – kilo, литр – liter, плане́та – planet, луна́ – moon, киломе́тр – kilometer
11 a3 television, b4 computer, c6 monitor, d5 notebook, e7 <u>lemonade</u>, f1 radio, g2 printer
12 1b park, 2f kiosk, 3l grocer's, 4g zoo, 5a stadium, 6i café, 7h sauna, 8d ATM, 9j institute, 10e casino, 11c theater, 12 (given in question) university, 13k antiques
14 lamp, chair, corridor, divan (sofa), mixer, vase, toaster, toilet, lift
15 saxophone, composer, guitar, piano, orchestra, soloist, opera, pianist, playlist, heavy metal, rock
16 menu, omelette, whisky, coffee, cutlet, cola
salad, fruit, muesli, wine, minestrone soup
17 a3, b6, c4, d1, e5, f2,
18 a5, b7, c8, d6, e1, f3, g2, h4
19 a5, b4, c10, d2, e12, f3, g14, h11, i9, j8, k1, l15, m6, n7, o13
20 a4 symphony, b5 ballet dancer, c7 poet, d2 actor (female), e1 bestseller, f8 actor (male), g3 ballet, h6 thriller
21 a4 energy, b5 kilowatt, c3 atmosphere, d1 kilogram, e6 electronics, f2 experiment

22 a2 souvenirs, b3 pet shop, c7 police, d5 driving school, e1 information, f4 pizza, g8 bank, h6 groceries
23 a manager, **b** conference, **c** briefing, **d** marketing, **e** playlist, **f** businessman, **g** know-how, **h** broker, **i** weekend, **j** computer, **k** notebook
25 Writers: a3, b2, c1, Composers: d2, e1, f3, Political leaders: g1, h3, i2

Part 2: Mechanics of the language

1 a (m), b (f), c (m), d (n), e (f), f (m), g (m), h (f), i (n), j (f), k (m), l (n)

UNIT 1

Russian names
1 Ivan, **2** Alexander

Vocabulary builder
Greetings: a Good day, **b** Good evening

Dialogues
Dialogue 1
1 Morning / Day / Evening / Any time / Any time
2 До́брое у́тро / До́брый ве́чер / Здра́вствуйте!/
До́брый день / До свида́ния
3 a до́брое у́тро, **b** до́брый ве́чер, **c** здра́вствуйте,
d до́брый день, **e** до свида́ния
Dialogue 2
1 Introducing themselves, **2** Good
Dialogue 3
1 Two people, **2** извини́те (excuse me)
Dialogue 4
1 Because Nikolai speaks English **2** To speak more slowly

Language discovery

a не, **b** говори́те, **c** пожа́луйста, **d** не/пло́хо

Your turn!
Здра́вствуйте, Валентина Ивановна!, Здра́вствуй, Коля!

Your turn!
1 a I know, **b** I understand, **c** I speak
2 a Я не зна́ю. **b** Я не понима́ю. **c** Я не говорю́.

Practice

1 a3, b1, c2, d4, e6, f5
Vladimir, Boris
2 a До́брое у́тро, **b** До́брый день, **c** До́брый ве́чер
3 a Меня́ зову́т ..., **b** О́чень прия́тно
4 e
6 a 3, **b** 5, **c** 2, **d** 1, **e** 4
7 a зову́т, **b** До́брый, **c** не, **d** говори́те, **e** челове́к
8 a 4, **b** 5, **c** 2, **d** 3, **e** 1

Listen and learn

1 c, **2** b, **3** c

Test yourself

1 a Hello, **b** Goodbye, **c** Excuse me, **d** What are you called?, **e** Do you speak English?
2 a Я не понима́ю., **b** ты, с вы, **d** О́чень прия́тно., **e** Ме́дленнее, пожа́луйста.

UNIT 2

Going places

Moscow is called the White Stone City because it was built in the 14th century from limestone. Limestone is white (or gray), so the Kremlin was white.

Language discovery

New expressions: Because they are describing nouns of different genders: masculine, feminine and neuter.

Dialogues

Dialogue 1

1 A bank, **2** Где? **3** Извини́те

Dialogue 2

1 Ко́смос, **2** The information office, **3** Спаси́бо

Dialogue 3

1 Finds out the options
2 a Restaurant, hotel, café, **b** Says извините (Excuse me), **c** Скажи́те, **d** Вот он / Вот она́ / Вот оно́.

Dialogue 4

1 Proud.
2 a Како́й э́то рестора́н? **b** Big theater, **c** пожа́луйста

Dialogue 5
1 Positive
2 a Big, good; **b** There is a lift, phone and beautiful balcony.
c Э́то ма́ленькая кварти́ра.
Dialogue 6
1 It is very small., **2** 1 d, 2 c, 3 a, 4 e, 5 b

Practice
2 a boulevard, **b** avenue, **c** campsite, **d** taxi rank, **e** café-bar, **f** tourist hotel, **g** botanical garden, **h** first-aid post, **i** yacht club, **j** tourist club, **k** canal, **l** Red Square, **m** swimming pool, **n** tourist agency
3 a он, **b** она́, **c** он, **d** оно́, **e** она́, **f** он, **g** она́, **h** оно́
5 a 2-6, **b** 7-5, **c** 3-4, **d** 8-1, **e** 10-0, **f** 9-10
6 a Вот оно́./Оно́ вон там. **b** Извини́те, я не зна́ю. **c** Нет, э́то по́чта.
d Не́ за что!
7 белая таблетка, зеленый салат, красное вино, черный кот, желтый банан

Test yourself
1 a trolleybus; **b** 3,5,10; **c** flat/apartment; **d** What sort of city is it?; **e** It's red wine.
2 a шесть, **b** два, **c** Где метро́? **d** Это банк? **e** Где рестора́н? Вот он.

UNIT 3

At the kiosk
map of Moscow

Dialogues
Dialogue 1
1 a young woman, **2** как попа́сть в ...? **3 a** T, **b** T, **c** F
Dialogue 2
1 Museum
2 И́горь, Музе́й недалеко́. Иди́те пря́мо, и музе́й напра́во.
3 Hello / museum / Is it...? / not far / interesting.
Dialogue 3
1 The museum is closed. **2 a** F, **b** F, **c** F
Dialogue 4
1 Russian dolls, postcards, samovar, Russian tea, Russian Faberge egg
2 in the bookstore
3 Russian chocolate

Language discovery
Your turn!
Куда́?, я иду́ , вы идёте

Practice

1 бана́ны, табле́тки, газеты и журналы, цветы́, конфе́ты, фру́кты

2 b Гузель краси́вая балери́на. **c** Хард-Рок америка́нское кафе́. **d** Ло́ндон большо́й го́род. **e** Коммерсант ру́сская газе́та.

5 a на по́чту, **b** в гости́ницу, **c** в поликли́нику, **d** на фа́брику

8 a, d

9 a 6, **b** 3/4, **c** 1, **d** 3, **e** 2, **f** 5

10 a ix, **b** xi, **c** vii, **d** i, **e** viii, **f** iv, **g** vi, **h** iii, **i** x, **j** ii, **k** v

11 a 2, **b** 5, **c** 3, **d** 1, **e** 4

Go further

1 a Телефо́н, **b** сим-ка́рта, **c** магазин, **d** Карина до́ма?

2 a 12-24-18, **b** 25-30-17, **c** 14-32-11, **d** 15-03-24, **e** 20-19-12

Test yourself

1 a How do I get to the center? **b** Do you have any flowers? **c** The museum is closed. **d** Repeat that, please. **e** Is it far?

2 a два́дцать шесть, трина́дцать, три́дцать, **b** рестора́ны, **c** Как попа́сть в музе́й? **d** Иди́те пря́мо. **e** Куда́ вы идёте?

UNIT 4

Shopping in Russia

supermarket and hypermarket

Vocabulary builder

New expressions: **1 a** tea with lemon, **b** coffee with milk

Dialogues

Dialogue 1

1 for souvenirs and gifts

Dialogue 2

1 Yes

2 a souvenirs and gifts, **b** gifts (e.g. dolls, books ...), **c** yes, **d** at the book shop ('House of the Book')

3 a yes, **b** the novel *Anna Karenina*. 550 roubles.

4 512 roubles

Dialogue 3

1 into a café

2 a fruit juice or tea, **b** mineral water and cola, **c** Peter: tea with lemon and sugar, Sofia: coffee with milk.

Dialogue 4

1 What have you got? **2** Music magazine 'Russian jazz', **3** She says they are very beautiful. **5** Tolstoy, Dostoyevsky, Chekhov, Gogol, Turgenev, Lermontov

Practice

1 a Где? **b** Как? **c** Куда́? **d** Что? **e** Кто?

2 b 1 Извините, нет; 2 Да, у нас ру́сские журналы.; 3 Да, у нас хоро́шие бана́ны.

3 a Повтори́те, **b** Покажи́те, **c** Дайте, **d** Иди́те, **e** Скажи́те, **f** Напиши́те, **g** Извини́те

4 a ва́ше моё, **b** ва́ша моя́, **c** ва́ши мои́, **d** ваш мой

5 Every item on the list is wanted.

fem: b во́дка, пи́цца; **c** смета́на; **d** Пепси-ко́ла

6 a Большо́й теа́тр, **b** ма́ленькое ра́дио, **c** краси́вые цветы́, **d** ру́сские журналы, **e** интере́сная кни́га, **f** молодо́й челове́к, **g** ботани́ческий сад, **h** хоро́шие конфе́ты, **i** бе́лое вино́.

7 a Я хочу́ чай с лимо́ном. **b** Я иду́ в кино́. **c** Это ру́сская во́дка. **d** Да, метро́ закры́то. **e** Да, э́то мой билет.

Test yourself

1 a What do you want to buy? **b** What have you got? **c** Show me, please. **d** How much does it cost? **e** Give me a coffee, please.

2 a чай с лимо́ном, **b** сто два́дцать, **c** мой па́спорт, **d** повтори́те, пожа́луйста, **e** молодо́й челове́к

UNIT 5

Hotel accommodation

c оте́ль (hotel)

Dialogues

Dialogue 1

1 Surname

2 a Как э́то пи́шется, Фио́на? (How is Fiona spelled?) **b** И кто вы по профе́ссии? (What do you do?) **c** Како́е у вас гражда́нство? (What nationality are you?) **d** У вас есть бага́ж? (Do you have luggage?)

3 passport, **4** suitcase, bag, accordion, **5** 38

Dialogue 2

1 TV, phone, balcony, shower, bathroom, toilet

2 Is there a restaurant? How do I get to the buffet? Where is the bar? The restaurant is closed.

3 To the buffet.

4 Sample questions **a** В номере есть душ? **b** В гостинице есть ресторан? с Где бар?

Dialogue 3

1 Say their profession, where they live and work.

Language discovery

If you say *at* or *in* a place, the ending changes to *e*.

Practice

2 a 2, **b** 4, **c** 6, **d** 1, **e** 3, **f** 5
3 a Scottish, **b** Portuguese, **c** Irish, **d** Norwegian
4 a ii 4 C, **b** iv 1 B, **c** i 2 A, **d** iii 3 D
5 a 3, **b** 5, **c** 2, **d** 7, **e** 1, **f** 4, **g** 6
6 a больни́це / Арха́нгельске, **b** стадио́не, **c** гости́нице, **d** рестора́не
7 a Э́та, **b** э́тот, **c** Э́ти, **d** э́то

Go further

1 a 7, **b** 11, **c** 8, **d** 9, **e** 1, **f** 5, **g** 2, **h** 10, **i** 3, **j** 6
2 f, c, e, d, h, a, g, b

Test yourself

1 a May I? **b** Where do you work? **c** I live in Moscow. **d** How is that written? **e** I'm Russian.
2 a Одну́ мину́точку. **b** Я рабо́таю в магази́не. **c** Вы говори́те по-англи́йски? **d** Магази́н откры́т? **e** пятьсо́т девяно́сто шесть.
3 a American (m), **b** German (m), **c** French (f), **d** Russian (m), **e** Japanese (f), **f** English (f)

UNIT 6

Breakfast, dinner, supper

black bread and white bread

Dialogues

Dialogue 1

1 three museums
2 Russian Museum, Pushkin Museum, Zoological Museum
3 a F, **b** T, **c** F

Dialogue 2

1 Go to concerts and films. **2** Start time and day.

Dialogue 3

1 Library
2 a 8.00, **b** 9.00, **c** at work

3 watch TV and go to bed late:
я смотрю́ телеви́зор и по́здно ложу́сь спать.

Dialogue 4

1 at the library
3 Встре́тимся, часо́в, в, Мо́жно
4 Где мы встре́тимся?

Language discovery

Practice

1 a 8.00, **b** 7.00, **c** 3.00, **d** 1.00, **e** 11.00, **f** 2.00, **g** 10.00, **h** 6.00, **i** 4.00
2 a Час, **b** Три часа́, **c** Пять часо́в, **d** Де́вять часо́в три́дцать мину́т, **e** Два часа́ со́рок пять мину́т, **f** Оди́ннадцать часо́в де́сять мину́т, **g** Двена́дцать часо́в пять мину́т, **h** Три часа́ два́дцать пять мину́т, **i** Четы́ре часа́ пятьдеся́т мину́т
3 a семь, встаю́, **b** во́семь, за́втракаю, **c** де́вять, иду́, **d** обе́даю, **e** во́семь, **f** де́вять, смотрю́, **g** оди́ннадцать
4 a Музе́й антрополо́гии и этногра́фии открыва́ется в оди́ннадцать часо́в. Выходно́й день – суббо́та. Телефо́н – две́сти восемна́дцать – четы́рнадцать – двена́дцать.
b Музе́й музыка́льных инструме́нтов открыва́ется в двена́дцать часо́в. Выходно́й день – вто́рник. Телефо́н – три́ста четы́рнадцать – пятьдеся́т три – пятьдеся́т пять.
c Музе́й-кварти́ра А. А. Бло́ка открыва́ется в оди́ннадцать часо́в. Выходно́й день – среда́. Телефо́н – сто трина́дцать – во́семьдесят шесть – три́дцать три.
d Музе́й А́рктики и Анта́рктики открыва́ется в де́сять часо́в. Выходно́й день – понеде́льник. Телефо́н – три́ста оди́ннадцать – два́дцать пять – со́рок де́вять.
5 a Чт. **b** Пн. **c** Вт. **d** Ср. **e** Сб. **f** Вс. **g** Пт.
6 a 1st (ground) floor, **b** 2nd, **c** 3rd, **d** 5th, **e** 5th, **f** 6th, **g** 4th **h** 5th **i** 2nd
7 a в теа́тре в Но́вгороде, **b** в библиоте́ку, **c** в университе́те, в шко́ле, **d** в институ́т, **e** в поликли́нику
8 a Wed, **b** Fri, **c** Tue, **d** Mon, **e** Thurs, **f** Sat, **g** Sun

Test yourself

1 a музе́й, **b** я встаю́, **c** конце́рт, **d** ка́ша, **e** спаси́бо, **f** хлеб
2 a понеде́льник, вто́рник, среда́, четве́рг, пя́тница, суббо́та, воскресе́нье (and then in reverse order). **c** Когда́ открыва́ется банк? **d** Когда́ начина́ется фильм? **e** Встре́тимся в семь часо́в в рестора́не. **f** porridge, muesli, bread, coffee, **g** Я встаю́ в семь часо́в. **h** Ве́чером я смотрю́ телеви́зор. **i** Я рабо́таю в Москве́. **j** Я иду́ в теа́тр.

UNIT 7

Public holidays

Russia Day, 12th June

Dialogues

Dialogue 1

1 Reading newspapers, books and Russian novels

2 я чита́ю газе́ты

3 No

4 sport: badminton, tennis, walking

5 Sample answer: Я люблю́ чита́ть журна́лы и игра́ть в футбо́л.

6 Jazz

7 I speak French

8 a That he is not Russian. **b** London **c** Avant-Garde Jazz concert **d** Here at six o'clock.

9 Let's meet at the bar in the hotel at seven o'clock.

10 b Я очень люблю теннис, книги и саксофон.

Language discovery

Я or a

Practice

1 a Thurs, **b** Wed, **c** Three sisters, **d** Tue

2 a 1 (In spring I like to travel.) **b** 3 (In summer I like to play tennis and read on the beach.) **c** 4 (In autumn I like to walk in the park.) **d** 2 (In winter I like to play ice hockey and watch TV.)

4 a Likes library, reading books, newspapers; **b** Plays badminton. Likes sport. Plays guitar; **c** Likes travel. Speaks English and French well. Doesn't like going to the opera or drinking champagne; **d** Likes going to theater and concerts. Likes music, plays balalaika. Likes pizza.

5 a пе́рвое января́, **b** седьмо́е января́, **c** восьмо́е ма́рта, **d** девя́тое ма́я, **e** (today's date), **f** (my birthday)

6 a трина́дцатое ию́ня, два́дцать четвёртого декабря́, три́дцать пе́рвое октября́; **b** шесто́е сентября́, тре́тье октября́, четырнадца́тое февраля́

7 a работаю, **b** говори́те, **c** понима́ю, **d** люблю́, **e** живёте, **f** за́втракаю, **g** гуля́ю

8

e, b Очень люблю́

c, f люблю́

a не люблю
d совсе́м не люблю́

Test yourself
2 a Reading papers, travel, music, going to concerts; **b** Reading, music.
c Sport, ice hockey in winter, walking in summer.

UNIT 8

Home and family
а кварти́ра

Dialogues
Dialogue 1
1 Two
Dialogue 2
1 Seryozha – flat, Tim – house, Bella – flat.
2 a wife, son, daughter, parents, brother, sister, uncle, aunt. **b** wife, children and parents are at the dacha. **c** student, **d** plays basketball, likes walking in country, **e** factory in Novosibirsk
3 a Bella, **b** Seryozha, **c** Tim

Practice
1 a Route 2 – 63 tram, **b** Route 3 – 28 bus, **c** Route 3 – 28 bus, **d** Route 1 – 17 trolleybus, **e** Route 3 – 28 bus, **f** Route 2 – 63 tram, **g** Route 1 – 17 trolleybus, **h** Route 3 – 28 bus
2
Anya: Moscow. Pharmacy. Mum and dad, sister. Cinema. Wants to speak German.
Peter: Bristol. Teacher, school. Son. Football. Wants to travel.
Leonid: Yekaterinburg. Train station. Wife. TV and sweets. Doesn't like sport. Wants to live in Moscow.
Zoe: St Petersburg. Ballerina. Theater. Husband and brother. Music. Wants to play piano.
3 живёт, магази́ны, ку́хня, её, лю́бит, день, хо́дит
4 Elite cottage. Prestige district. Electricity, water, gas. Jacuzzi and sauna. Fireplace. Satellite TV. 250 sq. m. Big garage.
5 a восто́ке, **b** за́паде, **c** ю́ге, **d** се́вере
6 Boris: Брат (brother), Кварти́ра (flat), **Nastya:** Кот (cat), Да́ча (dacha), **Liza:** Маши́на (car), Брат (brother), Кварти́ра (flat), Да́ча (dacha)
7 a зна́ю, **b** идёте, **c** хочу́, **d** говори́т, **e** рабо́таешь, **f** за́втракаю, **g** люблю́, **h** игра́ем, **i** у́жинают

Listen and understand
3 в теа́тр, по магази́нам, краси́вый

Test yourself
1 a read it **b** Moscow, **c** a train, **d** ordering a drink, **e** porridge, **f** a holiday, **g** a river, **h** the time, **i** 19th August, **j** Friday

UNIT 9

Souvenirs
tea with sugar and lemon

Vocabulary builder
Going round the shops: **1** grocery items: beer, bread, green tea, mineral water, pizza; non-grocery items: flowers, newspaper, jeans

Dialogues:
Dialogue 1
1 go shopping
2 a 9.00, **b** books, wooden toys, postcards, samovar, **c** not far, three stops on the bus, **d** opposite, **e** она́ говори́т, что, **f** The sales assistant's aunt lives in London and says that Russian samovars work there. **g** red, green, yellow.
3 a Хорошо́. **b** Вот э́ти?/Да, пожа́луйста
Dialogue 2
1 Cheese
2 a Мо́жно посмотре́ть? **b** Ско́лько вы хоти́те? **c** Всё? **d** здесь. **e** отде́л, **f** Ско́лько с меня́?

Language discovery
a Поня́тно, **b** Э́то недалеко́, **c** Кото́рый сейча́с час? **d** Хорошо́, **e** Вам помо́чь? **f** Отку́да вы? **g** Не волну́йтесь, **h** Да, коне́чно, **i** Повтори́те, пожа́луйста, ме́дленнее.

3 Where do you go?
cars, antiques, audio-video technical, bakery, grocer's, dietary products, design-studio, books, sausage, cosmetics, dairy products, musical instruments, meat, vegetables-fruit, optical, gifts, fish, sports goods, souvenirs, tobacco, flowers, clocks/watches.

Practice

1 books about sport

2 a lemons and mandarins, **b** gouda cheese from Holland, **c** ketchup, **d** Indian, **e** Stolichnaya, Smirnoff, Absolut

3 чай, огуре́ц, соси́ски, ба́нка ко́фе, кило́ помидо́ров, ры́ба, са́хар, колбаса́, конфе́ты, торт, буты́лка пи́ва.

4 coffee, fruit-flavoured water, vodka, fruit tea, champagne; sausage, chocolate, caramel, sauces, ketchups, sweets.

5 a У вас есть колбаса́? **b** ...чай? **c** ...торт? **d** ... ры́ба? **e** ...молоко́? **f** ...апельси́ны? **g** ... огурцы́?

6 a Matryoshka doll. Сувени́р. Straight ahead, on the left. **b** Books. Дом Кни́ги. Not far. Tram 31. 2 or 3 stops. **c** Cake. Grocer's У́лица Ми́ра.

Test yourself

1 a I'm listening, **b** Can I help you? **c** How much do you want? **d** These?

2 a Мо́жно посмотре́ть? **b** Покажи́те, **c** Ско́лько сто́ит? **d** У вас есть конфе́ты? **e** Это до́рого. **f** Повтори́те, пожа́луйста.

UNIT 10

On holiday

No spa or exercise room.

Dialogues

Dialogue 1

1 go skiing

2 a frosty and sunny, **b** watch TV and read, **c** summer. It's hot, can walk on beach and eat ice cream. **d** call Andrew, who likes winter sports. **e** 7391542.

Dialogue 2

1 to the theater

2 Helen is from Lancaster. Likes radio, chess, reading, films and concerts. Yura is from Krasnodar. Plays ice hockey, skis, walks in country, plays tennis, swims in sea, collects mushrooms.

3 Здесь мо́жно лови́ть ры́бу, купа́ться в мо́ре, загора́ть на пля́же, ката́ться на велосипе́де, ката́ться на ло́дке, игра́ть в те́ннис.

Language discovery

the phrase бу́дет

Practice

1 Tomorrow: **d** cold, **i** temperature –7°, **e** northerly wind, **b** snow, **g** frost
2 На за́паде па́смурно и идёт дождь. На се́вере тума́нно. На восто́ке ми́нус 10 гра́дусов и идёт снег. На ю́ге тепло́, плюс 20 гра́дусов и со́лнце све́тит.
3 a 3, **b** 4, **c** 2, **d** 5, **e** 1
4 a 3, **b** 1, **c** 2
5 Answers will vary. Sample answer: a1, b3, c7, d4, e2, f5, g6
6 a Sochi, in hotel at the beach. **b** Sunny and hot. **c** Eats ice cream and plays volleyball on the beach.
7 Sample answer:
Я хочу поехать в Сочи. Там красиво. Можно жить в отличной гостинице, ходить в хорошие рестораны и пить коктейли. Там всегда отличная погода, жарко и светит солнце. Море теплое и люди очень добрые.

Go further

a Моё люби́мое вре́мя го́да ... **b** Мой любимый спорт... **c** Моя́ люби́мая кни́га... **d** Моя́ люби́мая ма́рка маши́ны... **e** Мой люби́мые фи́льмы...
f Мой люби́мые компози́торы/спортсме́ны...

Test yourself

1 a What's the weather like today? **b** What's your favorite season? **c** What do you do in your free time? **d** It's raining. **e** Do you want to go to the cinema?
2 a С удово́льствием, **b** Я люблю́ смотре́ть фи́льмы.
c Сего́дня сли́шком жа́рко. **d** Мо́жно заказа́ть экску́рсию?
e Нет, я не о́чень хочу́. **f** За́втра бу́дет дождь.

Review units

R1

1 a До́брое у́тро. **b** До́брый день. **c** До́брый ве́чер. **d** Здра́вствуй! **e** До свида́ния.

2 a Где банк? Вот он. **b** Где гости́ница? Вот она́. **c** Где рестора́н? Вот он. **d** Где кафе́? Вот оно́.

3 a шесть, де́сять. **b** пятна́дцать, три́дцать. **c** оди́ннадцать, трина́дцать, семна́дцать.

4 a Музе́й откры́т? **b** Э́то далеко́? **c** Куда́ вы идёте? **d** У вас есть шокола́д? **e** Как попа́сть в Большо́й Теа́тр?

5 a Как попа́сть в библиоте́ку? **b** Как попа́сть в бассе́йн? **c** Как попа́сть в кафе́? **d** Как попа́сть на стадио́н?

6 a интере́сная – interesting book, **b** кра́сный – red bus, **c** ма́ленькое – small cafe.

R2

1 Do you have green tea?: У вас есть зелёный чай?
What do you have?: Что у вас есть?
Give me fruit juice, please: Да́йте, пожа́луйста, фрукто́вый сок.

2 a сто се́мьдесят два, со́рок пять, девяно́сто во́семь.
b три́ста трина́дцать, шестьдеся́т четы́ре, пятьдеся́т де́вять.
c пятьсо́т три́дцать шесть, четы́рнадцать, се́мьдесят два.
d восемьсо́т пятьдеся́т три, во́семьдесят оди́н, двена́дцать.

3 a Как? **b** Что? **c** Кто? **d** Где? **e** Когда́? **f** Куда́?

4 a ваш, мой; **b** моя́, ва́ша, моя́; **c** ва́ше, моё; **d** ва́ши, мои́

5 Answers will vary.

6 a University. Go straight ahead, then right. Not far. **b** Train station. Go to the left. 10 minutes away. **c** Library. There it is.

7 a Concert starts at 8.30. **b** Museum opens at 10.00. **c** Breakfast starts at 6.30. **d** On Monday the theater is closed.

8 a stadium 2.00, **b** hotel 8.00, **c** library 5.00, **d** café 1.00, **e** train station 4.00, **f** cinema 7.00

9 понеде́льник, вто́рник, среда́, четве́рг, пя́тница, суббо́та, воскресе́нье.

R3

1 a 1 Tue 8th April, **b** 1 Thurs 21st June, **c** 2 Sun 12th November, **d** 1 Sat 1st May, **e** 2 Wed 19th February

2 a живу́, **b** её, **c** рабо́тают

3 a Где вы живёте? **b** Где вы рабо́таете? **c** У вас есть хо́бби? **d** Вы лю́бите спорт? **e** У меня́ соба́ка. **f** У тебя́ есть брат? **g** У них больша́я кварти́ра. **h** Э́то её па́спорт? **i** Она́ лю́бит её? **j** Он хорошо́ говори́т по-ру́сски.
4 a оте́ц, **b** мать, **c** муж, **d** жена́, **e** приёмный сын, **f** дочь, **g** брат, **h** сестра́, **i** тётя, **j** дя́дя, **k** де́душка, **l** ба́бушка.
5 a Show me, **b** Repeat, **c** Write, **d** Don't worry, **e** Slower, **f** Give me.
6 a Мо́жно посмотре́ть? **b** Ско́лько сто́ит? **c** Это до́рого. **d** Мо́жно? **e** Всё, спаси́бо. **f** У вас есть чёрный хлеб?
7 a I'm listening. b Is that all? **c** Can I help you? **d** How much do you want? **e** Understood. **f** Here you can buy fruit and vegetables. **g** What do you want? **h** These sweets cost 370 roubles. **i** Which ones? **j** Of course.
8 a 2 Today it's cold and windy. It's raining. **b** 2 Today it's too hot. It's plus 30 and close. **c** 1 Tomorrow there will be snow and frost.
9 a 1 Winter. Skiing in the forest. **b** 2 Autumn, collecting mushrooms. **c** 1 Summer. Holidays abroad, sunbathing on the beach, swimming in the sea. **d** Spring. Riding a bicycle. Sunny but cool.
10 a Я совсе́м не люблю́ смотре́ть телеви́зор. **b** Что вы де́лаете в свобо́дное вре́мя? **c** Ле́том я бу́ду в Москве́. **d** Ты хо́чешь пойти́ в парк за́втра у́тром?

Summary of language patterns

THE/A

There are no words in Russian for *the* and *a*.

TO BE

The verb *to be* is not used in the present tense.

SPELLING RULES

1 Do not use ы after г, к, х, ж, ч, ш, щ. Instead, use и.

2 Do not use unstressed о after ж, ч, ш, щ, ц. Instead, use е.

GENDER OF SINGULAR NOUNS

Masculine nouns end in a consonant: парк; й музе́й; ь Кремль

Feminine nouns end in а: река́; я эне́ргия; ь дочь

Neuter nouns end in о: метро́; е кафе́

PLURAL FORMS OF NOUNS

Masculine: рестора́н/рестора́ны *restaurant/s*; кио́ск/кио́ски *kiosk/s*; рубль/рубли́ *rouble/s*

Feminine: гости́ница/гости́ницы *hotel/s*; библиоте́ка/библиоте́ки *library/libraries*; пло́щадь/пло́щади *square/s*

Neuter: у́тро/у́тра *morning/s*

Many neuter nouns (кино́, метро́, пиани́но, ра́дио) do not change.

ADJECTIVES

Masculine singular	Это краси́**вый** парк.	*It's a beautiful park.*
Feminine singular	Это краси́**вая** ва́за.	*It's a beautiful vase.*
Neuter singular	Это краси́**вое** ра́дио.	*It's a beautiful radio.*
Plural	Это краси́**вые** ма́рки.	*They are beautiful stamps.*

Most common endings: -ый -ий -ой (m), -ая -яя (f), -ое -ее (n) -ые -ие (pl).

POSSESSIVE PRONOUNS

Мой (*my/mine*), твой (*your/yours*), наш (*our/ours*), ваш (*your/yours*) change form to agree with nouns to which they refer.

Masculine	**Feminine**	**Neuter**	**Plural**
мой па́спорт	моя́ балала́йка	моё пиани́но	мои́ де́ньги
твой па́спорт	твоя́ балала́йка	твоё пиани́но	твои́ де́ньги
наш па́спорт	на́ша балала́йка	на́ше пиани́но	на́ши де́ньги
ваш па́спорт	ва́ша балала́йка	ва́ше пиани́но	ва́ши де́ньги

Его́ (*his*), её (*her/hers*), их (*their/theirs*) do not change form.

его́ па́спорт, его́ балала́йка, его́ пиани́но, его́ де́ньги

PRONOUNS

Где авто́бус?	*Where is the bus?*	Вот он.	*There it is.* (m)
Где ва́за?	*Where is the vase?*	Вот она́.	*There it is.* (f)
Где ра́дио?	*Where is the radio?*	Вот оно́.	*There it is.* (n)
Где конфе́ты?	*Where are the sweets?*	Вот они́.	*There they are.* (pl)

DEMONSTRATIVE PRONOUNS

Да́йте, пожа́луйста, э́тот чемода́н.	*Please give me that suitcase.*
Э́та де́вушка – моя́ дочь.	*This girl is my daughter.*
Покажи́те, пожа́луйста, э́то ра́дио.	*Please show me that radio.*
Э́ти биле́ты – мои́.	*These tickets are mine.*

PERSONAL PRONOUNS

Singular: я *I*; ты *you* (informal); он *he/it*; она́ *she/it*; оно́ *it*

Plural: мы *we*; вы *you* (plural or formal); они́ *they*

As well as meaning *his*, *her* and *their*, the words его, её and их mean *him*, *her* and *them* in phrases where personal pronouns are the direct object of the verb.

ты лю́бишь меня́	*you love me*	вы лю́бите нас	*you love us*
я люблю́ тебя́	*I love you*	они́ лю́бят вас	*they love you*
она́ лю́бит его́	*she loves him*	мы лю́бим их	*we love them*
он лю́бит её	*he loves her*		

TO HAVE

Singular: у меня́ *I have*; у тебя́ *you have*; у него́ *he/it has*; у неё *she has*

Plural: у нас *we have*; у вас *you have*; у них *they have*

ACCUSATIVE CASE AFTER Б AND X (*INTO/TO*)

Masculine and neuter singular nouns do not change after в and на when motion is indicated; feminine singular nouns change their endings from -а to -у and -я to -ю.

Masculine	**Feminine**	**Neuter**
Как попа́сть в теа́тр?	**Как попа́сть на по́чту?**	**Как попа́сть в кафе́?**

ACCUSATIVE CASE WITH DIRECT OBJECTS

The accusative case is used when an inanimate noun is the direct object of a verb. Only the feminine singular ending changes.

Я люблю́ спорт.	*I love sport.* (m)
Я люблю́ му́зыку.	*I love music.* (f)
Я люблю́ кино́.	*I love cinema.* (n)
Я люблю́ кни́ги.	*I love books.* (pl)

PREPOSITIONAL CASE AFTER Б AND X (*IN*)

When в and на mean *in* or *at* a certain place, they trigger the prepositional case in the following word.

Masculine	**Feminine**	**Neuter**
(институ́т) в институ́те	**(шко́ла) в шко́ле**	**(письмо́) в письме́**
(Кремль) в Кремле́		
(музе́й) в музе́е		

VERBS IN PRESENT TENSE:

Group 1 verbs

рабо́тать *to work*

я рабо́таю	мы рабо́таем
ты рабо́таешь	вы рабо́таете
он/она́/оно́ рабо́тает	они́ рабо́тают

идти́ *to go on foot* **(on one occasion)**

я иду́	мы идём
ты идёшь	вы идёте
он/она́ идёт	они́ иду́т

быть *to be* **(future tense)**

я бу́ду	мы бу́дем
ты бу́дешь	вы бу́дете
он/она́ бу́дет	они́ бу́дут

пить *to drink*

я пью	мы пьём
ты пьёшь	вы пьёте
он/она́ пьёт	они́ пьют

мочь *to be able*

я могу́	мы мо́жем
ты мо́жешь	вы мо́жете
он/она́ мо́жет	они́ мо́гут

Group 2 verbs

говори́ть *to speak/talk*

я говорю́	мы говори́м
ты говори́шь	вы говори́те
он/она́ говори́т	они́ говоря́т

ходи́ть *to go on foot* **(habitually)**

я хожу́	мы хо́дим
ты хо́дишь	вы хо́дите
он/она́ хо́дит	они́ хо́дят

люби́ть *to love*

я люблю́	мы лю́бим
ты лю́бишь	вы лю́бите
он/она́ лю́бит	они́ лю́бят

Irregular verbs

хоте́ть *to want*

я хочу́	мы хоти́м
ты хо́чешь	вы хоти́те
он/она́ хо́чет	они́ хотя́т

есть *to eat*

я ем	мы еди́м
ты ешь	вы еди́те
он/она́ ест	они́ едя́т

Russian–English glossary

а	*but*
а́вгуст	*August*
авто́бус	*bus*
автомоби́ль (m)	*car*
администра́тор	*administrator*
а́дрес	*address*
алло́	*hello (on phone)*
альбо́м	*album*
апельси́н	*orange*
апте́ка	*pharmacy*
атле́тика	*athletics*
аэропо́рт	*airport*
ба́бушка	*grandmother*
бага́ж	*luggage*
банк	*bank*
бар	*bar*
бассе́йн	*swimming pool*
бе́лый	*white*
бери́те	*take (imperative)*
(не) беспоко́йтесь	*(don't) worry (imperative)*
библиоте́ка	*library*
бизнесме́н	*business person*
биле́т	*ticket*
бланк	*form*
большо́й	*big*
брат	*brother*
бу́дет	*will be*
бу́лочная	*bakery*
бульва́р	*boulevard*
буты́лка	*bottle*
быть	*to be*
бюро́ обслу́живания	*service desk*
в	*in, into*
ва́нная	*bathroom*
вас	*you (object)*
ваш	*your*
весна́	*spring*
ве́трено	*windy*

вид	*view*
ви́деть 2 (ви́жу, ви́дишь)	*to see*
ви́за	*visa*
вку́сный	*tasty*
вода́	*water*
во́здух	*air*
вокза́л (на)	*train station*
воскресе́нье	*Sunday*
восто́к (на)	*east*
вот	*there*
врач	*doctor*
вре́мя	*time*
всё	*everything*
всегда́	*always*
встаю́	*I get up.*
вто́рник	*Tuesday*
вход	*entrance*
вчера́	*yesterday*
вы	*you (pl, formal)*
высо́кий	*tall*
вы́ход	*exit*
выходи́ть	*to go out*
газе́та	*newspaper*
галере́я	*gallery*
гарни́р	*side dishes*
гастроно́м	*grocer's*
где	*where*
глаз	*eye*
говори́ть 2	*to say, talk*
год	*year*
голубо́й	*blue*
го́род	*town*
горя́чий	*hot*
господи́н	*Mr;* *госпожа́ Mrs, Miss*
гости́ница	*hotel*
гото́вить 2 (гото́влю, гото́вишь)	*to prepare, cook*
гражда́нство	*nationality*
гуля́ть 1	*to go for a walk*
да	*yes*
да́йте	*give (imperative)*
далеко́	*far, a long way*
да́ча	*dacha (country house)*
дверь (f)	*door*

де́вушка	*girl, young woman*
де́душка	*grandfather*
дека́брь (m)	*December*
де́лать 1	*to do*
де́ньги	*money*
де́ти	*children*
до свида́ния	*goodbye*
до́брое у́тро	*good morning*
до́брый ве́чер	*good evening*
до́брый день	*good day*
дово́льно	*fairly, quite*
дождь (m)	*rain*
до́ктор	*doctor*
докуме́нт	*document*
дом	*house, block of flats*
дочь (f)	*daughter*
ду́мать 1	*to think*
душ	*shower*
дя́дя	*uncle*
ёлка	*fir tree*
если	*if*
есть	*there is, there are*
есть	*to eat*
ехать 1 (еду, едешь)	*to go by transport*
ещё	*another*
ждать 1 (жду, ждёшь)	*to wait*
жёлтый	*yellow*
жена́	*wife*
же́нщина	*woman*
жить 1 (живу́, живёшь)	*to live*
журна́л	*magazine*
за грани́цей	*abroad*
за́втра	*tomorrow*
за́втрак	*breakfast*
заказа́ть	*to order*
закры́т	*closed*
за́пад (на)	*west*
запо́лните	*fill in (imperative)*
здесь	*here*
здра́вствуйте	*hello*
зелёный	*green*
зима́	*winter*
знать 1	*to know*

зоопа́рк	*zoo*
и	*and*
игра́ть 1	*to play*
игру́шка	*toy*
иди́те	*go (imperative)*
извини́те	*excuse me (imperative)*
или	*or*
имя	*name*
инжене́р	*engineer*
институ́т	*institute*
интере́сный	*interesting*
информа́ция	*information*
ию́ль (m)	*July*
ию́нь (m)	*June*
к себе́	*pull*
к сожале́нию	*unfortunately*
к сча́стью	*fortunately*
ка́ждый	*each, every*
ка́жется	*it seems*
как	*how*
кака́о	*cocoa*
кани́кулы	*school holidays*
ка́сса	*cash desk*
кафе́	*café*
кварти́ра	*flat*
кино́	*cinema*
кио́ск	*kiosk*
кли́мат	*climate*
ключ	*key*
кни́га	*book*
код	*code*
ко́мната	*room*
компью́тер	*computer*
кому́	*to whom*
коне́чно	*of course*
консье́рж	*concierge*
конфе́та	*sweet*
коридо́р	*corridor*
костю́м	*suit*
кот	*cat*
ко́ттедж	*cottage*
ко́фе	*coffee*
краси́вый	*beautiful*

кра́сный	*red*
кто	*who*
куда́	*where to*
купа́ться	*to swim*
купи́ть	*to buy*
ку́хня	*kitchen*
ла́дно	*OK*
ла́мпа	*lamp*
ле́вый	*left*
лека́рство	*medicine*
лес	*forest*
ле́то	*summer*
лифт	*lift*
лу́чше	*better*
люби́мый	*favorite*
люби́ть 2 (люблю́, лю́бишь)	*to love*
магази́н	*shop*
май	*May*
ма́ленький	*small*
ма́льчик	*boy*
ма́ма	*mum*
март	*March*
маршру́т	*route*
ма́сло	*butter*
мать (f)	*mother*
маши́на	*car*
ме́дленнее	*slower*
ме́неджер	*manager*
меню́	*menu*
меня́	*me*
ме́сто	*place, seat*
ме́сяц	*month*
метро́	*metro*
минера́льная вода́	*mineral water*
мину́та	*minute*
мно́го	*a lot*
моби́льный телефо́н	*mobile phone*
мо́жет быть	*maybe*
мой	*my*
молодо́й	*young*
молоко́	*milk*
моло́чные проду́кты	*dairy products*
монито́р	*monitor*

мо́ре	*sea*
моро́женое	*ice cream*
моро́з	*frost*
мост	*bridge*
мочь 1 (могу́, мо́жешь)	*to be able*
мужчи́на	*man*
музе́й	*museum*
му́зыка	*music*
мы	*we*
мы́ло	*soap*
мя́гкий	*soft*
мя́со	*meat*
на	*at, to, on*
на́до	*it's necessary*
нале́во	*to the left*
напи́ток	*drink*
напиши́те	*write (imperative)*
напра́во	*to the right*
напро́тив	*opposite*
наш	*our*
не	*not*
недалеко́	*not far*
неде́ля	*week*
некраси́вый	*ugly*
немно́жко	*a little bit*
нет	*no*
но	*but*
но́вый	*new*
но́мер	*number, hotel room*
норма́льно	*all right, fine*
но́утбук	*notebook (computer)*
ноя́брь (m)	*November*
о	*about*
обе́д	*dinner*
обме́н валю́ты	*currency exchange*
объе́кт	*object*
обы́чно	*usually*
о́вощи	*vegetables*
одну́ мину́точку	*wait a minute*
окно́	*window*
октя́брь (m)	*October*
он	*he, it*
она́	*she, it*

они́	*they*
оно́	*it*
о́сень (f)	*autumn*
остано́вка	*stop (bus)*
от себя́	*push*
отде́л	*department*
отдыха́ть 1	*to rest, holiday*
оте́ц	*father*
откро́йте	*open (imperative)*
откры́т	*open*
откры́тка	*postcard*
отку́да	*where from*
о́тпуск	*holiday*
о́тчество	*patronymic name*
официа́нт, официа́нтка	*server (m/f)*
о́чень	*very*
о́чередь (f)	*queue*
пальто́	*coat*
па́па	*dad*
парк	*park*
па́спорт	*passport*
пассажи́р	*passenger*
пи́во	*beer*
письмо́	*letter*
пить 1 (пью, пьёшь)	*to drink*
пи́цца	*pizza*
пишу́	*I write*
план	*plan*
плане́та	*planet*
плати́ть	*to pay*
пло́хо	*it's bad*
пло́щадь (f) (на)	*square*
плюс	*plus*
по	*by, on, at, along*
повтори́те	*repeat (imperative)*
пого́да	*weather*
пода́рок	*present*
по́дпись (f)	*signature*
по́езд	*train*
пожа́луйста	*please*
пожа́р	*fire*
пожило́й	*elderly*
позвони́ть	*to phone*

по́здно	*it's late*
покажи́те	*show (imperative)*
по́лдень (m)	*midday*
поликли́ника	*health center*
по́лночь (f)	*midnight*
полоте́нце	*towel*
помидо́р	*tomato*
понеде́льник	*Monday*
понима́ть 1	*to understand*
попа́сть	*to get to*
пора́	*it's time*
посмотре́ть	*to have a look*
посмотри́те	*look (imperative)*
(мы) потеря́ли	*(we) lost*
пото́м	*then*
потому́, что	*because*
по́чта (на)	*post office*
пра́вильно	*that's right*
пра́вый	*right*
пра́здник	*public holiday, festive occasion*
прекра́сный	*fine (adj)*
прести́жный райо́н	*prestige district*
принести́	*to bring*
принима́ть 1 (лека́рство)	*to take (medicine)*
при́нтер	*printer*
проводни́к, проводни́ца	*conductor (m/f)*
прогно́з	*forecast*
продаве́ц, продавщи́ца	*shop assistant (m, f)*
продаётся, продаю́тся	*is for sale, are for sale*
проду́кты	*groceries*
(у меня́) пропа́л	*(I've) lost*
проспе́кт	*avenue*
профе́ссия	*profession*
пря́мо	*straight ahead*
путеше́ствовать	*to travel*
пье́са	*play*
пя́тница	*Friday*
рабо́та (на)	*work*
рабо́тать 1	*to work*
ра́дио	*radio*
раз	*once, time*
ра́но	*early*
расписа́ние	*timetable*

река́	*river*
(вы) рекоменду́ете	*(you) recommend*
реко́рд	*record*
ре́мни	*seat belts*
рестора́н	*restaurant*
рис	*rice*
рисова́ть	*to draw*
рождество́	*Christmas*
рот	*mouth*
рубль (m)	*rouble*
ры́ба	*fish*
ры́нок	*market*
с	*with*
с удово́льствием	*with pleasure*
сад	*garden*
сади́тесь	*sit down (imperative)*
сала́т	*salad*
самолёт	*airplane*
са́хар	*sugar*
се́вер (на)	*north*
сего́дня	*today*
сейча́с	*now*
семья́	*family*
сентя́брь (m)	*September*
се́рый	*gray*
серьёзный	*serious*
сестра́	*sister*
скажи́те	*say, tell me (imperative)*
ско́лько	*how much, how many*
сли́шком	*too, too much*
слу́шать 1	*to listen*
смета́на	*sour cream*
смотре́ть 2	*to look, watch*
снег	*snow*
собира́ть 1	*to collect*
совсе́м	*quite, entirely*
спаси́бо	*thank you*
спать	*to sleep*
спина́	*back*
споко́йной но́чи	*good night*
спорт	*sport*
спра́вочное бюро́	*information bureau*
спу́тниковое ТВ	*satellite TV*

среда́	*Wednesday*
стадио́н (на)	*stadium*
стака́н	*glass*
ста́нция (на)	*station (metro)*
старт	*start*
ста́рый	*old*
стол	*table*
столо́вая	*dining room*
стоп	*stop*
студе́нт, студе́нтка	*student (m, f)*
стул	*chair*
суббо́та	*Saturday*
сувени́р	*souvenir*
су́мка	*bag*
суп	*soup*
суперма́ркет	*supermarket*
счёт	*bill, check*
сын	*son*
сыр	*cheese*
сюда́	*here (motion)*
таба́к	*tobacco*
табле́тка	*tablet*
так	*so*
такси́	*taxi*
тало́н	*ticket (transport)*
там	*there*
теа́тр	*theater*
текст	*text*
телеви́зор	*television*
телефо́н	*phone*
тёмный	*dark*
температу́ра	*temperature*
те́ннис	*tennis*
теря́ть	*to lose*
тётя	*aunt*
ти́хо	*it's quiet*
то́же	*also*
то́лько	*only*
торго́вый центр	*shopping center*
торт	*cake*
то́стер	*toaster*
трамва́й	*tram*
тра́нспорт	*transport*

тролле́йбус	*trolleybus*
туале́т	*toilet*
тума́нно	*it's foggy, misty*
тури́ст, тури́стка	*tourist (m, f)*
туристи́ческое аге́нтство	*tourist agency*
ты	*you (singular, informal)*
ужа́сный	*awful*
уже́	*already*
у́жин	*supper*
у́лица (на)	*street*
универма́г	*department store*
универса́м	*supermarket*
университе́т	*university*
уста́л	*tired*
у́хо, у́ши	*ear, ears*
учи́тель, учи́тельница	*teacher (m, f)*
фа́брика (на)	*factory*
фами́лия	*surname*
февра́ль (m)	*February*
фунт сте́рлингов	*pound sterling*
хи́мик	*chemist*
хлеб	*bread*
холо́дный	*cold*
хоро́ший	*good*
цветы́	*flowers*
центр	*center*
це́рковь (f)	*church*
цирк	*circus*
ци́фры	*numbers*
чай	*tea*
час	*hour, o'clock*
ча́сто	*often*
часы́	*watch, clock*
чек	*receipt*
челове́к	*man, person*
чемода́н	*suitcase*
че́рез	*after*
чёрный	*black*
четве́рг	*Thursday*
число́	*number, date*
чита́ть 1	*to read*
что	*what, that*
ша́пка	*hat*

шко́ла	*school*
экску́рсия	*excursion*
экспре́сс	*express*
электри́чка	*suburban train*
электро́ника	*electronics*
эта́ж	*floor, storey*
э́та, э́тот,; э́ти	*this (f, m); these*
юг (на)	*south*
я	*I*
янва́рь (m)	*January*

Transliteration appendix

UNIT 1

Dialogue 1 (01.02)

Véektor Dóbroye óotra, Natásha.
Natásha Dóbroye óotra, Véektor.
Barées Dóbry dyen', Ánna.
Anna Dóbry dyen', Barées.
Svyéta Dóbry vyécher, Lyéna.
Lyéna Dóbry vyécher, Svyéta.
Iréena Zdrástvooeetyi!
Antón Zdrástvooeetyi!
Tánya Da sveedánya, Eeván.
Eeván Da sveedánya, Tánya.

Dialogue 2 (01.03)

Igor' Dóbry vyécher. Minyá zavóot Igor'.
Alison Óchen' preeyátna.
Igor' Kak vas zavóot?
Alison Minyá zavóot Álison.
Igor' Ochen' preeyátna. Kak dyilá, Álison?
Alison Khurashó, spaséeba.

Dialogue 3 (01.04)

Valódya Eezveenéetye, maladóy chilavyék, vy Sásha?
Méesha Nyet, ya nye Sásha.
Valódya Eezveenéetye ... dyévushka, vy nye Nástya?
Vyéra Nástya? Net, ya nye Nástya.
Valódya Eezveenéetye, vy Sásha ee Nástya?
Sásha Da, vy Valódya?
Valódya Da, ya Valódya. Óchen' preeyátna, Sásha. Óchen' preeyátna, Nástya.

Dialogue 4 (01.05)

Nikalái Zdrástvooeetyi.
Andrew Zdrástvooeetyi.
Nikalái Kak vas zavóot?
Andrew Myédlyn-ye-ye, pazháloosta.
Nikalái Kak vas zavóot?

Andrew	Eezveenéetye. Ya nye paneemáyoo.
Nikalái	Kak vas zavóot? Minyá zavóot Nikalái Pitróvich. Kak vas zavóot?
Andrew	A, minyá zavóot Andrew. Vy gavaréetye pa-angléesky?
Nikalái	Da, ya gavaryóo pa-angléesky.
Andrew	Oh good! Khurashó! Ya plókha paneemáyoo pa-róosky.

UNIT 2

Dialogue 1 (02.02)

Andrew	Eezveenéetye, pazháloosta, Éto bank?
Muscovite	Nyet, Éto póchta.
Andrew	Gdye bank?
Muscovite	Bank von tam.

Dialogue 2 (02.03)

Andrew	Éto keenotiátr 'Kósmos'?
Muscovite	Nyet, éto keenotiátr 'Planyéta'.
Andrew	Gdye keenotiátr 'Kósmos'?
Muscovite	Eezveenéetye, ya nye znáyoo.
Andrew	Gdye správuchnoye byuró?
Muscovite	Von tam.
Andrew	Spaséeba.
Muscovite	Nyé za shto! Da sveedánya.

Dialogue 3 (02.04)

Andrew	Eezveenéetye, gdye zdyes' ristarán?
Muscovite	Vot on.
Andrew	Skazhéetye, pazháloosta, gdye zdyes' gastéeneetsa?
Muscovite	Vot aná.
Andrew	Spaséeba. Gdye zdyes' kafé?
Muscovite	Vot anó.

Dialogue 4 (02.05)

Andrew	Skazhéetye, kakóy éto górat?
Muscovite	Éto bal'shóy, kraséevy górat.

Dialogue 5 (02.06)

Valodya	Skazheetye, kakaya eto kvarteera?
Sasha	Eto bol'shaya, kharoshaya kvarteera. Tam lift, vanaya ee kraseevyi balkon.

Dialogue 6 (02.07)

Valodya	Eto ochen' malen'kaya kvarteera.
Sasha	Nyet, eto nye malen'kaya kvarteera. Kvarteera - bal'shaya, kraseevaya.

UNIT 3

Dialogue 1 (03.02)

Andrew	Dyévooshka, eezveenéetye, kak papást' v tsentr?
Young woman	V tsentr? Eedéetye pryáma, patóm nalyéva, ee tam Krásnaya plóshshad' ee kryeml'.
Andrew	Pavtaréetye, pazháloosta.
Young woman	Eedéetye pryáma, patóm nalyéva.
Andrew	Spaséeba.

Dialogue 2 (03.03)

Igor'	Zdrástvooeetyi, Álison. Koodá vy eedyótye?
Alison	Ya eedóo v moozyéy. Éto dalyikó?
Igor'	Net, eto nidalyikó. Eedéetye pryáma, ee moozyéy naprάva. Moozyéy óchen' intiryésny.
Alison	Spaséeba. Da sveedánya.

Dialogue 3 (03.04)

Igor'	Álison, moozyéy zakrýt. Zakrýt na rimónt.
Alison	Oy, kak zhal'!
Igor'	No galiryéya atkrýta. Ee galiryéya óchen' intiryésnaya.
Alison	Kak papást' v galiryéyoo?
Igor'	Eedéetye nalyéva, patóm naprάva, ee galiryéya pryáma. Eto nidalyikó.

Dialogue 4 (03.05)

Kai	Oo vas yest' soovinéery?
Kiosk keeper	Da. Vot matryóshky ee kanfyéty. Zdyes' kompákt-déesky ee tam róoskaya vótka ee róoskoe vinó.
Kai	Eto róosky shakalát?
Kiosk keeper	Nyet, amirikánsky. Ochen' kharóshy shakalát.
Kai	A oo vas yest' knéegy?
Kiosk keeper	Nyet, eedéetye v Dom Knéegy. Eto nidalyikó.
Kai	Gdye Dom Knéegy?
Kiosk keeper	Eedéetye nal**y**´eva, patom pryáma, ee Dom Knéegy naprάva.

Dialogue 1 (04.02)

Sofia Ivanova Shto vy khatéetye koopéet', Péeter?
Peter Soovinéery ee padárky.
Sofia Ivanova Kakéeye soovinéery ee padárky?
Peter Ya khachóo koopéet' knéegy, matryóshky, shakalát, vódkoo ee balaláikoo.
Sofia Ivanova Kharashó. Paeedyóm v Dom Kneegy.

Dialogue 2 (04.03)

Peter Oo vas yest' knéega 'Anna Karyénina'?
Young man Da.
Peter Pukazhéetye, pazháloosta.
Young man Vot aná.
Peter Skól'ka stóeet?
Young man Sto pidisyát rooblyéi.
Peter Gdye platéet'?
Young man Eedéetye v kásoo.
Peter Spaséeba.

Dialogue 3 (04.04)

Sofia Ivanova Shto vy khatéetye, Péeter?
Peter Ya khachóo frooktóvy sok eely chai, pazhaáloosta.
Sofia Ivanova Dyévooshka, eedéetye syoodá, pazháloosta. Oo vas yest' frooktóvy sok?
Server Eezveeneetye, nyet.
Sofia Ivanova Shto oo vas yest?
Server Chai, kófye, minirál'naya vadá, pepsi-kóla.
Peter Dáitye, pazháloosta, chai s leemónum ee s sákharum.
Sofia Ivanova Ee kófye s mulakóm.
Server Chai s leemónum ee s sákharum, ee kófye s mulakóm. Seychás.

Dialogue 4 (04.05)

Sofia Ivanova Shto oo vas yest?
Peter Vot knéega Ánna Karyénina' ee matryóshky.
Sofia Ivanova Kak khurashó. Eto óchen' kraséeveeye matryóshky. Peter, éto vash kompákt-déesk?
Peter Da. Eto moy kompákt-déesk, 'Róosky dzhaz'.
Sofia Ivanova Ee vot moy kompákt-déesk. Opyira 'Barées Gadoonóf'.
Server Vot chai ee kófye.

Peter Spaséeba.
Sofia Ivanova Oh look, it's twelve o'clock. We can speak English now!

UNIT 5

Dialogue 1 (05.02)

Fiona Zdrástvooeetyi.
Administrator Adnóo minóotuchkoo. Da, slóoshayoo vas.
Fiona Minyá zavóot Fióna Hárrison. Ya khachóo kómnatoo, pazháloosta.
Administrator (*looks through bookings*) Fióna Hárrison? Da, vot vásha faméeliya. Vásha kómnata nómyer tréedtsat' vósyim.
Fiona Spaséeba.
Administrator Zapólneetye étot blank.
Fiona (*handing the form to the administrator for help*) Mózhna, pazháloosta? Ya gavaryóo pa-róosky, no plókha peeshóo.
Administrator Mózhna. Kak vásha faméeliya?
Fiona Faméeliya Hárrison, ee éemya Fióna.
Administrator Tak, Hárrison. Kak éto péeshetsa, Fióna?
Fiona F-ee-o-n-a.
Administrator Kakóy oo vas ádryis?
Fiona Ángleeya, Shelton, Oóleetsa Crossley, dom treenádtsat'.
Administrator Ee kto vy pa prafyéssee?
Fiona Ya oochéetyelneetsa. Ya rabótayoo v shkólye v Sheltonye.
Administrator Kakóe oo vas grazhdánstva?
Fiona Ya angleechánka.
Administrator Vash páspurt, pazháloosta.
Fiona Vot on.
Administrator Spaséeba. Oo vas yest' bagásh?
Fiona Da, vot moy chimadán, mayá sóomka ee moy akordeón.
Administrator Vot vash klyooch.

Dialogue 2 (05.03)

Administrator Vot vásha kómnata. Vot oo vas tyilyivéezur, tyilyifón ee balkón. Ee v kareedórye doosh, vánnaya ee tooalyét.
Fiona Spaséeba. Skazhéetye, v gastéeneetse yest' ristarán?
Administrator Da, ristarán, boofyét ee bar. No ristarán seychas zakrýt.
Fiona Kak zhal'! Kak papást' v boofyét?
Administrator Boofyét naprάva. Éto nidalyekó.
Fiona Ee bar?
Administrator Bar vneezóo.

Dialogue 3 (05.05)

Fiona	Kto vy pa prafyéssee? Gdye vy zheevyótye ee gdye vy rabótayete?
Jomo	Minyá zavóot Dzhomo. Ya eenzhinyér. Ya rabótayoo v eensteetóotye v Berléenye. Ya nyémyets.
Brigitte	Zdrastvooéetyi, minyá zavóot Brigitte. Ya frantsóozhenka. Ya oochéetyelneetsa ee ya zheevóo v Lyonye. Ya tam rabótayoo v shkólye.
Sergéi	Minyá zavóot Sergéi. Ya pradavyéts ee ya rabótayoo v magazéenye zdyes' v Maskvyé. Ya, kanyéshna, róosky.
Greg	Zdrastvooéetyi, ya amyirikányets ee minyá zavóot Greg. Ya aktyór ee ya zheevóo v New Yorkye.
Iréena	Ya vrach. Minyá zavóot Iréena. Ya rabótayoo v paleekléeneekye v Nóvgaradye. Ya róoskaya.
Juanita	Minyá zavóot Juanita. Ya pradavshshéetsa ee rabótayoo v magazéenye. Ya zheevóo v Barselónye. Ya eespánka.

UNIT 6

Dialogue 1 (06.02)

Steven	Kagdá atkriváyetsa róosky moozyéy?
Marat	Róosky moozyéy atkriváyetsa v dyésyat' chasóf. Vykhadnóy dyen' – ftórneek.
Steven	Ee moozyéy-kvartéera Póoshkina?
Marat	Adnóo minóotuchkoo. Da, moozyéy-kvartéera Póoshkina atkriváyetsa v dyésyat' chasóf. Vykhadnóy dyen' – sryidá.
Steven	Ee kagdá atkriváyetsa za-alagéechesky moozyéy?
Marat	Za-alagéechesky moozyéy atkriváyetsa pózdna, v adéenadtsat' chasóf. Vykhadnóy dyen' – pyátneetsa.

Dialogue 2 (06.03)

Steven	Kagdá nachináyetsa kantsyért?
Marat	Kantsyért v chitvyérk. On nachináyetsa rána, v shest' chasóf.
Steven	Ee kagdá nachináyetsa feel'm?
Marat	Kázhdy dyen' feel'm nachináyetsa v chitýrye chasá.

Dialogue 3 (06.04)

Marat	Oótrum ya fstayóo v vósyem' chasóf ee záftrakayoo v dyévyat' chasóf. Patóm ya eedóo na rabótoo v beebleeotyékoo. Beebleeotyéka atkriváyetsa v dyésyat' chasóf. Ya tam abyédayoo, ee vyéchirom ya óozhinayoo v syem' chasóf. Patóm ya smatryóo tyilyivéezur ee pózdna lazhóos' spat'.

Dialogue 4 (06.06)

Steven Gdye my fstryétimsa?

Marat Kantsyért nachináyetsa v shest' chasóf v zálye Feelarmónee. Fstryétimsa v pyat' chasóf v beebliotyékye . Mózhna, Steven?

Steven Mózhna.

UNIT 7

Dialogue 1 (07.02)

(Part A)

Lyudméela Kakéeye oo vas khóbbee?

George Ya óchen' lyooblyóo cheetát'.

Lyudméela Cheetát'? Kakéeye knéegy vy cheetáyetye?

George Kázhdy dyen' ya cheetáyoo gazyéty, ee ya tózhe lyooblyóo cheetát' ramány.

Lyudméela Intiryésna. Vy lyóobeetye róoskeeye ramány?

George Da, óchen' lyooblyóo. A vy, oo vas yest' khóbbee?

Lyudméela Da, no ya savsyém nye lyooblyóo cheetát'. Ya lyooblyóo sport. Ya eegráyoo v badmeentón ee v tyénnis, ee ya lyooblyóo goolyát'.

(Part B)

George Vy lyóobeetye móozykoo?

Lyudméela Da, ya óchen' lyooblyóo dzhaz.

George Ya tózhe. Ya eegráyoo na saksafónye. V Lóndonye ya óchen' lyooblyóo khadéet' na kantsyérty.

Lyudméela V Lóndonye? Skazhéetye, vy nye róosky?

George Nyet, ya angleechánin. Ya zheevóo v Lóndonye.

Lyudméela Vy khurashó gavaréetye pa-róosky.

George Spaséeba. Ya gavaryóo pa-róosky ee pa-frantsóosky, ee ya óchen' lyooblyóo pootyishéstvuvat'.

Lyudméela Intiryésna. Dzhordzh, vy lyóobeetye dzhaz ee sivódnya pyátoye aktyabryá. Sivódnya vyéchirom ya eedóo na kantsyért – Déekseelend. Vy khatéetye paeetée na kantsyért?

George Da, kanyéshna ya khachóo. Spaséeba. Kagdá nachináyetsa kantsyért?

Lyudméela V syem' chasóf. Fstryétimsa zdyes' v shest' chasóf.

George Khurashó. Spaséeba, Lyudméela.

Lyudméela Pazháloosta.

Dialogue 1 (08.02)

Nikalái Vkhadéetye, Sállee! Minyá zavóot Nikalái.

Sally Óchen' preeyátna, Nikalái.

Nikalái Óchen' preeyátna, Sállee. Sadéetyes', pazháloosta.

Sally Eezveenéetye! Skazhéetye, oo vas yest' sim'yá?

Nikalái Da, yest'. Pasmatréetye, oo minyá zdyes' al'bóm. Éto mayá zhiná, ee vot dyétee, véedeetye? Oo minyá syn ee doch'. Eekh zavóot Alyósha ee Léeza. Alyósha óchen' lyóobeet mashéeny ee Léeza lyóobeet sport. Zhiná – oochéetyel'neetsa. Yiyó zavóot Gálya. Zhiná ee dyétee seychás na dáche.

Sally Na dáche? Kak khurashó. A kto éto? Mat' ee atyéts?

Nikalái Da, éto máma ee pápa. Anée na pyénseeee, ee lyétum anée zhivóot na dáche. Ya eekh óchen' lyooblyóo. A vot moy brat. Yivó zavóot Véektor. On stoodyént, khurashó gavaréet pa-nimyétsky ee pa-angléesky ee khóchet pootyishéstvuvat'.

Sally Intiryésna ...

Nikalái Ee vot mayá sistrá. Yiyó zavóot Éera. Aná óchen' inyergéechnaya dyévooshka, eegráyet v basketból ee lyóobeet goolyát' v dyiryévnye. Ee vot dyádya ee tyótya. Anée inzhinyéry, rabótayoot na fábreekye v Novaseebéersky.

Dialogue 2 (08.04)

Siryózha Ya zhivóo v kvartéerye na Oóleetse Méera. Oo nas v kvartéerye gastéenaya, spál'nya, kóokhnya, vánnaya ee balkón. Kvartéera nóvaya, ee oo nas yest' leeft ee tyilyifón. A gdye vy zhivyótye, Tim?

Tim Ya zhivóo v dómye v Leevyerpóolye. Éto stáry, bal'shóy dom. Oo nas bal'sháya gastéenaya, prikrásnaya stalóvaya, mályin'kaya kóokhnya, tree spál'nee ee vánnaya.

Siryózha Oo vas yest' sat?

Tim Da, oo nas bal'shóy sat. Násha sabáka, Tréeksee, lyóobeet tam eegrát'.

Bélla Oo minyá stáraya kvartéera v dómye na ryiké Móikye. Aná kraséevaya. Oo minyá v kvartéerye gastéenaya, kabeenyét, kóokhnya ee vánnaya. Oo minyá prikrásny veet na ryikóo Móikoo. Tam tak preeyátna.

Dialogue 3 (08.09)

You Pachyemoo vy lyoobeetye zhit' v goradye?

Anna Ya lyooblyoo zhit' v goradye patamoo chto mooozhno khadeet' na kantserty, v teatr, v kino, pa magazeenam. Nash gorad eestareecheskyi, kraseevyi. My zhivyom v tsentrye i u nas yest' stantsiya metro nedalyeko.

You Sasha, pachemoo vy lyoobitye zhit' v direvnye?

Sasha Ya lyooblyoo zhit' v direvnye patamoo chto tam spakoino i mozhna goolyat' v lyesoo. Priyezshaitye k nam v gosti. V derevnye ochen' priyatno.

UNIT 9

Dialogue 1 (09.02)

Chris Ya sivódnya khachóo khadéet' pa magazéenam.

Alyék Shto ty khóchesh' koopéet'?

Chris Padárky ee soovyinéery. Ya khachóo koopéet' knéegy, dyiryivyáneeye eegróoshky, atkréetky ee samavár. Ya óchen' lyooblyóo chai s leemónum.

Alyék Panyátna. Knéegy ee atkrýtky pradayóotsa v magazéenye 'Dom Knéegy'. Éto nyidalyikó.

Chris A gdye pradayóotsa samaváry ee eegróoshky?

Alyék V magazéenye 'Róoskee sóovyinéer. Katóry seychás chas?

Chris Dyévyat' chasóf.

Alyék Khurashó. 'Dom Knéegy' atkriváyetsa v dyévyat' chasóf.

Chris Kak papást' v 'Dom Knéegy'?

Alyék Tree astanófkee na avtóboosye. Astanófka tam, napróteef.

(Later, in 'Rooskee soovyineer')

Saleswoman Vam pamóch'?

Chris Pazháloosta, da! Pukazhéetye, pazháloosta, étot samavár. Nyet, vot étot. Alyék, kakóy éto kraséevy samavár! Dyévooshka, éto ilyiktréechesky samavár?

Saleswoman Da, ilyiktréechesky. Atkóoda vy?

Chris Ya angleechánka, zhivóo v Lóndonye.

Saleswoman Nye valnóoeetyes'. Mayá tyótya zhivyót v Lóndonye, ee aná gavaréet, shto náshee samaváry khurashó tam rabótayoot.

Chris Panyátna. Pukazhéetye, pazháloosta, étee dyirivyánneeye eegróoshky. Da, krásneeye ee zilyóneeye. Ee vot étee zhólteeye.

Saleswoman Vot étee?

Chris Da. Spaséeba. Napeeshéetye, pazháloosta, skól'ka anée stóyat.

Dialogue 2 (09.03)

Saleswoman	Slóoshayoo vas.
Nick	Oo vas yest' syr?
Saleswoman	Yest' lee oo nas syr? Da, kanyéshna. Vot on.
Nick	Kakóy éto syr? Mózhna pasmatryét', pazháloosta?
Saleswoman	Mózhna. Éto estónsky syr. Stóeet dvyéstee rooblyéy keeló.
Nick	Puvtaréetye, pazháloosta, myédlyinye-ye.
Saleswoman	Dvyéstee rooblyéy.
Nick	Éto dóraga?
Saleswoman	Nyet, nyidóraga. Skól'ka vy khatéetye?
Nick	Pit'sót gram. Skól'ka s minyá?
Saleswoman	Sto rooblyéy. Fsyo?
Nick	Da, fsyo. Gdye platéet'?
Saleswoman	V kássoo.
Nick	A gdye kássa?
Saleswoman	Napróteef. Véedeetye?
Nick	Da. Spaséeba. Kakóy zdyes' atdyél?
Saleswoman	Chitvyórty.

UNIT 10

Dialogue 1 (10.02)

Rosemary	Makséem, ty khóchesh' sivódnya katát'sa na lýzhakh v lyisóo?
Makséem	Nyet, nye óchen' khachóo. Sivódnya khóludna.
Rosemary	Kanyéshna khóludna! Zeemá! No sivódnya tak prikrásna. Maróz ee sólntse svyéteet.
Makséem	Da, no pa rádeeo gavaryát, shto timpiratóora vózdookha sivódnya méenoos dyésyat' grádoosuv. Sléeshkum khóludna. Ya khachóo smatryét' tyilyivéezur ee cheetát' dóma, gdye tyipló.
Rosemary	Smatryét' tyilyivéezur? Makséem, shto ty! Kak éto mózhet byt'? Ty savsyém nye lyóobeesh' zeemóo?
Makséem	Nyet, ya lyooblyóo lyéta, kagdá zhárka. Mózhna goolyát' na plyázhe ee yest' marózhenoye.
Rosemary	Panyátna. Ya tózhe óchen' lyooblyóo lyéta. No ya tak khachóo sivódnya katát'sa na lýzhakh. Zhal'. Shto dyélat'?
Makséem	Mózhna pazvanéet Ándryoo. On óchen' lyóobeet zéemnee sport.

Rosemary	Práveel'na. Nádu pazvanéet Ándryoo. Kakóy oo nyivó nómyer tyilyifóna?
Makséém	Syem'sót tréetsat' dyévyat', pitnátsat', sóruk dva.

Dialogue 2 (10.04)

Helen	Kakéeye oo tibyá khóbbee?
Yóora	Ya óchen' aktéevny chilavyék. Zeemóy ya lyooblyóo eegrát' v khakéi ee katát'sa na lýzhakh, a lyétum ya chásta goolyáyoo v dyiryévnye ee eegráyoo v tyénees. Ya tózhe lyooblyóo koopát'sa v mórye. Ósyin'yoo ya sabeeráyoo greebý v lyesóo. A oo tibyá yest' khóbbee?
Helen	Da, no ya nye óchen' aktéevny chilavyék. Ya lyooblyóo slóoshat' rádeeo, eegrát' v shákhmaty, cheetát' knéegy, smatryét' féel'my ee khadéet' na kantsyérty.
Yóora	V Lankástrye yest' tiátr?
Helen	Kanyéshna yest'. No ya nye óchen' chásta khazhóo v tiátr v Lankástrye patamóo shto dóruga stóeet.
Yóora	Da, panyátna. Zdyes' v Krasnadárye oo nas kharósheeye tiátry. Ty khóchesh' paeetée v tiátr záftra vyéchirom?
Helen	Da, s oodavól'stveeyem!

Practice

Exercise 4

Mini dialogues (10.06)

a

Young woman	Váshee beelyéty, pazháloosta.
Ványa	Adnóo meenóotuchkoo. Vot anée.
Young woman	Khatéetye pragrámoo?
Ványa	Da. DáItye, pazháloosta, tree pragrámy.

b

Lára	Skazhéetye, pazháloosta, kagdá eedyót ballet "Zheezyél"?
Kiosk keeper	Vas'móva, divyátuva ee disyátuva apryélya.

c

Gálya	Oo minyá yest' beelyéty v Bal'shóy tiátr. Vy svabódny?
Charles	Kanyéshna. Kak khurashó! Beelyéty na sivódnya?
Gálya	Da, na sivódnya na vyéchir.
Charles	Gdye my fstryéteemsa?
Gálya	Oo minyá v kvartéerye v shest' chasóf.

Can-do statements

UNIT	CEFR level	ACTFL level	CAN-DO STATEMENTS
UNIT 1	**A1**	**Novice High**	I can make an introduction by asking and answering questions about personal details such as someone's name, occupation and nationality. I can exchange and understand basic greeting and leave taking expressions.
UNIT 2	**A1 / A2**	**Novice High / Intermediate Low**	(A2) I can understand sentences and frequently used expressions describing relatives by name, age and occupation. (A1) I can deal with numbers to count family members and state people's ages.
UNIT 3	**A1 / A2**	**Novice High / Intermediate Low**	(A1) I can understand and use basic phrases to describe the date, time and today's weather. (A2) I can deal with numbers using various counters such as years of age, hours and minutes.
UNIT 4	**A1**	**Novice High**	I can understand and use simple sentences to ask for items in a shop. I can handle numbers to state prices and quantities.

UNIT	CEFR level	ACTFL level	CAN-DO STATEMENTS
UNIT 5	**A1 / A2**	**Novice High / Intermediate Low**	(A2) I can understand and use common expressions for ordering and dining in a restaurant. (A1) I can use basic phrases to describe and comment on a meal.
UNIT 6	**A1 / A2**	**Novice High / Intermediate Low**	(A1) I can recognize and use basic phrases describing a location in relation to its surroundings. (A2) I can ask for and give directions to a point of interest using frequently used expressions.
UNIT 7	**A1 / A2**	**Novice High / Intermediate Low**	(A2) I can understand and give instructions for traveling via various modes of transport to reach a destination. (A1) I can recognize and use basic phrases to compare different routes and state the time it takes.
UNIT 8	**A1**	**Novice High**	I can recognize and use basic phrases to list hobbies, likes and dislikes. I can understand simple expressions to describe the frequency one does a hobby or sport.
UNIT 9	**A1**	**Novice High**	I can form simple sentences in past tense to describe activities done in the past. I can recognize and understand basic expressions to describe a day in the past.

UNIT	CEFR level	ACTFL level	CAN-DO STATEMENTS
UNIT 10	**A1**	**Novice High**	I can form simple sentences using the future tense to describe activities that will be done in the future. I can recognize and understand basic expressions to make an appointment to meet in the future.

Dear Reader,

We'd love your attention for one more page to tell you about the crisis in children's reading, and what we can all do.

Studies have shown that reading for fun is the **single biggest predictor of a child's future life chances** – more than family circumstance, parents' educational background or income. It improves academic results, mental health, wealth, communication skills, ambition and happiness.[1]

The number of children reading for fun is in rapid decline. Young people have a lot of competition for their time. In 2024, 1 in 10 children and young people in the UK aged 5 to 18 did not own a single book at home.[2]

Hachette works extensively with schools, libraries and literacy charities, but here are some ways we can all raise more readers:

- Reading to children for just 10 minutes a day makes a difference
- Don't give up if children aren't regular readers – there will be books for them!
- Visit bookshops and libraries to get recommendations
- Encourage them to listen to audiobooks
- Support school libraries
- Give books as gifts

There's a lot more information about how to encourage children to read on our website: **www.RaisingReaders.co.uk**

Thank you for reading.

hachette UK

---

[1] National Literacy Trust, Book Ownership in 2024, November 2024 https://nlt.cdn.ngo/media/documents/Book_ownership_in_2024

[2] OECD. 2021. 21st-century readers: developing literacy skills in a digital world. Paris, France: OECD Publishing.
https://www.oecd.org/en/publications/21st-century-readers_a83d84cb-en.html

Notes